FRONTIER TALES OF TENNESSEE

Happy Birthday Carlton,

Christine

Also by Louise Littleton Davis

More Tales of Tennessee (1976)
Nashville Tales (1981)

Frontier Tales
of
Tennessee

Louise Littleton Davis

PELICAN PUBLISHING COMPANY
GRETNA 1983

First printing, October 1976
Second printing, December 1978
First paperback printing, October 1983

Library of Congress Cataloging in Publication Data

Davis, Louise Littleton.
   Frontier Tales of Tennessee.

      Bibliography.
      Includes index.
      CONTENTS: Sam Houston and his tragic marriage.—
Aaron Burr was framed.—Lincoya, old Andy's little
Indian. [etc.]
         1. Tennessee—History—Addresses, essays, lectures.
      2. Tennessee—Biography. 3. United States—Biography.
      I. Title.
      F436.D38   976.8   76-18122
      ISBN 0-88289-422-6

Manufactured in the United States of America

Published by Pelican Publishing Company, Inc.
1101 Monroe Street, Gretna, Louisiana 70053

Contents

Out of the pages of the *Tennessean Magazine* (Sunday supplement of the Nashville *Tennessean*) for many years have stepped some of the most fascinating characters in American history. And out of the readers' fascination with those characters has come this constant request: "Why don't you publish those stories in book form, so that we can read them again and keep them more easily?"

This Bicentennial era seems the appropriate time. Here at last is a collection of some of the favorites that readers have requested (excluding those of purely local interest). All of the characters, from Sam Houston and the tragic marriage that led him to new adventures, to the mysterious Melungeons in the mountains of East Tennessee, are unique in American history.

Much of the material gathered here has never been published before. Some of the information comes from family documents, or from interviews with descendants of the people involved. For stories about people living today, like the Melungeons, the stories represent days of interviewing the people involved and the people who have grown up around them. This alone meant weeks of probing, finding ways of overcoming long-standing barriers between them and the "outsider."

Though the adventures gathered here are centered in the South and in Tennessee, they reach in influence to all parts of the nation. There are stories of ruthless politics and personal tragedy—as in the case of Aaron Burr, the brilliant New Yorker for whom the times were wrong; and "Black Horse Harry" Lee, the Virginian of distinguished family who managed to muddle it all.

There are stories of high courage and adventure on ocean and river, on three-masted brig and river steamboat; on Pitcairn Island among the descendants of the mutineers from the *Bounty*; and in Memphis in 1878, when the nation's worst epidemic of yellow fever rode the steamboats up the Mississippi.

There are stories of triumph and ingenuity like that of Matthew Fontaine Maury, who turned his misfortune into opportunity to probe the ocean's depths and pave the way for much of today's weather forecasts, for transatlantic communication, for submarine exploration under the North Pole, and for mapping the ocean floors.

The stories range in time from the stouthearted settlers who fought their way through Indian attack and political scheming, to today's Melungeons—rapidly disappearing from the high ridges and deep hollows between East Tennessee mountains.

Some of the characters, like Andrew Jackson, turn up repeatedly in a variety of settings. Their life in the newly cleared forests and along the river banks was rough, whether in the struggle for survival itself or for some chance at pushing civilization westward.

Notable in this Bicentennial era, there was plucky, stubborn Capt. William Driver, a young sea captain from Salem, Massachusetts, whose conquest of icy storms off the frozen coast of New England was preparation for his wild adventures in the tropic South Pacific. His adventures there and in many distant ports pressed on his mind indelibly the protective power of our flag.

It was Driver who, out of a grateful heart, named the flag "Old Glory." He cherished it so intensely that he risked becoming an outcast in his Tennessee home by flying it during the Civil War. Nothing in this world was so precious to him as the Union, symbolized by Old Glory. For that he cut himself off from sons, friends, fellow citizens.

FRONTIER TALES OF TENNESSEE

Sam Houston and the Mystery of His Tragic Marriage

No other governor's race in Tennessee has ended as explosively, as mysteriously, as tragically as Sam Houston's— abruptly cut off the same week it began one April day in 1829. No governor's name has ever been entwined in a romance as baffling or as haunting as the one that ended Houston's marriage that same day. And no secret has been better kept than the one that Sam Houston and his bride, a beautiful blue-eyed Gallatin girl named Eliza Allen, took to their graves.

Yet now a yellowed letter, with pale ink fading almost to a shadow, has come out of a Gallatin attic to throw the brightest beam so far on the mystery. The speculation, the insinuations, the whispered scandals that neither Houston nor his departed bride condescended to answer begin to fall into their proper place. The rumors that trailed Houston through anguished exile among the Indians, through almost superhuman feats in war and peace to found Texas, through some of the most dramatic moments in the history of the United States, take on another color now.

A giant of a man (he stood six feet, six inches in his socks, a long-time friend said), young Houston first burst on the Nashville scene in all the splendor of his cherished uniform as second lieutenant in the U.S. Army. That was in 1816, when Houston was twenty-three years old and still aching from the wounds of fierce combat. Even then he had a sweetheart back in Knoxville. One admirer called her the "Princess of East Tennessee" and reported she was eager to desert home, mother, and all other suitors to follow Houston "to earth's remotest bounds." But Sam shied away. He had resolved long before not to "court any of the Dear Girlies before I make a fortune." He asked for and got a transfer to Washington.

Already an aura of mystery surrounded the elusive young man who had disappeared from civilization, during his adolescence, to "live among the Indians." A moody youth, son of a dashing army officer with extravagant tastes and an aristocratic mother with a fortune of her own, Sam Houston shared his father's distaste for farm life. But he had a special nostalgia for the Virginia home, near Lexington, where he was born March 2, 1793, and lived until he was fourteen. His father died that year, after running through his own sizable inheritance and his wife's, but he had made provision for the family to move "out West," near Maryville, Tennessee, and there the tall, brave widow took her nine children to start a new life.

Young Sam, fifth son in the family, was impatient with the drudgery of clearing new farm land. He was indifferent to school, but he read the ancient classics from his father's library: Homer's *Iliad* and other tales of ancient valor. And he was fascinated with the mysterious ways of the Cherokees, whose settlement lay just three miles from his mother's farm. Three times he slipped away from home to live among the Indians for a year. Once when his older brothers came to get him, they found him lying under a tree on the island in the Tennessee where the Cherokee chief had his wigwam. Sam was reading the *Iliad*.

The peace of the place and the freedom from white men's tasks made him adamant to his brother's pleas to come home. He hunted and fished with the Cherokees, learned their language and dances, played their games, and was admitted to their secret religious ceremonies. The spirit world that filled Indian lore intrigued him, and the incantations that summoned spirits to "heal" the sick cast their everlasting spell over him. He fell in love and learned the rigid protocol of Cherokee courtship. He was at last adopted by the Indian chief, Oo-loo-te-ka, and was given the Indian name that meant "The Raven."

But he was a disgrace to his family in Maryville, his brothers felt. His mother grieved for her "black sheep," the handsomest of her six sons. When he reappeared at her door briefly during his three years of self-imposed exile, she outfitted him in new clothes and saw to it that he was made presentable.

Sam was sixteen years old when he went to live with the Cherokees, eighteen when he returned to Maryville to clerk for a while in a store owned by his mother and then to organize and teach a private school. Maryville people thought it a great joke when wayward Sam, who had been a shameless truant, announced he would teach school; but his father's library had given him sound knowledge, and his skill as a disciplinarian brought him quick success. The little log schoolhouse, five miles from Maryville, was crowded with pupils at fifteen dollars' tuition per pupil, and Sam paid off his debts.

In later life, when Houston had been governor of two states, United States senator, and conquering general in a war with Mexico, he said he had never experienced more power than in that classroom. Standing before his pupils with a "sour wood" stick in his hand—unmistakable emblem of authority—Houston, "dressed in hunting shirt of flowered calico, a long queue down my back," experienced a "higher feeling of dignity and self-satisfaction than from any office or honor which I have since held."

His wild youth, he had decided, was behind him. But the War of 1812 began in June, 1812, just a month after Houston's school opened, and a year later, on March 24, 1813, he stood on a Maryville street corner and watched a recruiting parade. The drum and fife were playing, and all a man had to do to "join up" was step forward and pick up one of the silver dollars lying on the drumhead. Clothes-conscious Sam, eyeing the snappy uniform of blue waistcoat and white pantaloons, stepped out into the street, picked up his silver dollar, and fell into step in the procession. He was in the United States Army.

Just past his twentieth birthday, Sam had to have his mother's consent. The gallant Elizabeth Houston not only gave her consent, but she placed on his finger a ring that would give him something to live by the rest of his life. Inside the ring that he wore to his grave was engraved the one word "Honor." Sam resolved that Blount County would hear great things of him yet.

The following January, after training in Knoxville, Sam got his first orders: his outfit, the Thirty-ninth Infantry, would march to Fort Strother, in Alabama, not to fight the British but to fight the Creeks, who were siding with the British. When the 350 well-disciplined men of the Thirty-ninth Infantry marched into Fort Strother on a cold, rainy February day in 1814, they could hardly have found a more dismal scene. Gen. Andrew Jackson was in serious trouble with his own men. After winning two battles over the Creeks, some of the two thousand Tennessee militia had turned tail and run home. Others were threatening mutiny. All were miserably cold and hungry.

Ens. Sam Houston was leading his platoon as they marched

into Fort Strother, and the effect of the "regulars" on morale was instant. In six weeks Jackson had whipped his militia into shape and marched them, in ten days, through fifty-five miles of wilderness to attack the Creeks in a well-fortified bend of the Tallapoosa River, near the present Montgomery, Alabama. As it turned out, this bloody battle at Horseshoe Bend was the most crucial encounter with the Creeks, and leaving its cruel mark on young Houston for life, it shaped his role in history.

It was March 27, 1814, and at 10 A.M. Jackson's two little cannons began firing at the tight band of breastworks the Indians had built to seal themselves inside the horseshoe bend in the river. By early afternoon, after a brief truce to evacuate Indian women and children, Jackson's army gave the signal that the battle was on for keeps.

The regulars were first to charge the rampart. First man over was Maj. Lemuel P. Montgomery, the man for whom Montgomery, Alabama, is named. He fell back dead. Next man over was Ens. Sam Houston, the man for whom Houston, Texas, is named. Waving his sword, Houston leaped down among the Creeks, signaling his platoon to follow—they found him covered with blood, beating Indians off with a sword. Suddenly Jackson's men had the Indians on the run, but Houston stood in agony with a barbed arrow buried deep in his flesh. Some historians have said the arrow was in his thigh, but a Nashville physician of the day, Dr. W. D. Haggard, said the arrow ripped through the groin, tearing through part of the intestine.

At any rate, Houston yelled to a nearby lieutenant to pull the arrow out. The officer tried, but the arrow held tight. Wild with pain, Houston threatened to kill the officer if he did not pull with all his might. The officer braced himself, tugged mightily, and tore the arrow out, leaving a hideous wound that plagued Houston the rest of his life. Stunned and bleeding heavily, he limped through the battle-field to find the surgeons, and they plugged up the wound, which was never to heal completely.

As Houston lay under a tree "to steady himself," General Jackson rode by and ordered him not to return to battle. Houston said later that he would have obeyed if he had not remembered his vow to do something Blount County would hear about. The opportunity came by mid-afternoon. All of the Creeks had been killed except a small band hidden in a covered redoubt at the bottom of a deep ravine. Jackson called for volunteers to rout them. There was a silence, and then Houston, calling to his men, led the attack.

Over the rampart he scrambled, down the steep bank, musket leveled at the portholes of the enemy. The Indians held their fire until the rash, and perhaps feverish, Houston was within five yards. When they let go with their volleys, one ball shattered his right arm and another smashed his right shoulder. Houston's men deserted him, and he collapsed as he tried to crawl back up the ravine.

Jackson set fire to the Indian hideout with flaming arrows, and the Creek part of the fighting for England was over. But Houston's fame had just begun. General Jackson never forgot the raw courage of the youth who had offered his life twice in one horribly bloody afternoon.

Houston said later he did not know how he survived the sixty-mile ride on a sapling litter through swamp and forest to the nearest fort. But there was no medical care and only the roughest food there. So a sapling litter was strung between two horses to jog him across Alabama and most of Tennessee to his mother's home at Maryville. Houston was delirious much of the time. To make matters worse, he had the measles. By the time he reached his mother's home, in May, 1814, two months after the battle, Houston was so emaciated, so changed, that she did not recognize him at first. Only by the expression in his eyes did she finally know him.

Two months of devoted care put Houston on his feet again, and he got on a horse to ride off to Washington, arriving just in time to see the ruins of the White House the British had burned. In a rage at not being able to fight again, Houston did get to rejoin his regiment in Tennessee the next winter. There he got word of Jackson's stunning victory at the Battle of New Orleans on January 8, 1815. Soon after that, Houston was ordered to New Orleans, where army doctors decided to remove the ball the Creeks had buried in his shoulder. The surgery nearly killed him, and he was sent to New York for treatment.

In the spring of 1816, on a furlough to his mother's home in Tennessee, he met the Knoxville girl, "the Princess of East Tennessee," identified only as "Miss M." It was then that he was assigned to duty in Nashville, and had word from a go-between that the girl was eager to marry him. Soon afterward he was assigned to duty as an Indian agent, negotiating with the Cherokees for American land rights.

In that job, decked out in the Indian garb he loved, Houston accompanied a delegation of Cherokee chieftains to Washington in February, 1818, to sign agreements with the War Department. John C. Calhoun, secretary of war and a brittle stickler for formality, bawled Houston out for appearing before him "dressed as a savage," and a few days later accused Houston of dishonesty in a transaction with the Indians—an accusation that Houston immediately proved to be not only without basis, but a cover-up for those who were guilty. Calhoun made no effort to punish the real culprits, and Houston, in a white fury, resigned his commission and returned to civilian life to study law in Nashville. From that day on, his career shot forward. In six months he had completed an eighteen-month law course and passed the state bar exam. In Lebanon, where he opened his first law office and practiced for a year, his striking wardrobe ("plum-colored coat, tight breeches, colorful waistcoats"), his "pleasant ways," and his "rich, warm voice" made an instant hit. When he left to become a district attorney general in Nashville, a crowd of well-wishers gathered on the courthouse steps at Lebanon to tell him good-bye and hear his farewell speech.

After a year on the job in Nashville, the popular Houston resigned to reenter private practice. He was rising fast in state politics, and he and his good friend, Gov. William Carroll, were much in the company of Andrew Jackson, a power in national politics. Houston lived at the Nashville Inn, on the north side of the public square, and Jackson held court here almost daily. There gentlemen were challenged to duels. Houston won his, over a political controversy with Gen. William A. White, a Nashville lawyer. At sunup the two parties met in a pasture just over the Kentucky line. Houston fired and White fell.

"General, you have killed me," White said.

"I am very sorry," Houston replied. "But you know it was forced upon me."

"I know it, and forgive you."

But White recovered. And Jackson decided to back Houston for Congress. He won, in 1823.

In Washington, Houston sat up all night, swapping political gossip with the nation's great, by the fireside in cozy taverns. Or he walked till dawn, talking with friends. No one knew then that the all-night ramblings were shadows of the fears that haunted Houston all his life—a man afraid of nothing in the daylight, but afraid to be alone in the dark of night. He was much in demand socially, and one of the many Washington belles he squired was Mary Custis, the heiress who lived in the great mansion at Arlington and later married Gen. Robert E. Lee.

By the time Houston returned to Nashville to run for governor in 1827, he was a national figure. His military bearing, his "courtly manners and magnetism" earned him "unbounded popularity among men" and made him "a great favorite with the ladies." On election day, riding to the polling places in his white ruffled shirt, "shining" black trousers, beaded red sash, and silver-buckled shoes, "on a superb dapple-gray horse," he made an unforgettable picture. He won the election easily.

An aristocratic young lady from South Carolina, in Nashville on her wedding trip, found the whole city "in great excitement" over "a great parade on the day of the entrance of their new Governor."

"He is the most popular man in the State," Juliana Courtney Conner wrote in her diary on Friday, June 21, 1827. "His rapid and unparalleled rise is sufficient evidence of the fact. . . . He is said to be a very elegant man in his appearance."

When Juliana danced with Houston a few nights later, at the most fashionable wedding of the season, she was charmed by the dashing bachelor governor-elect. "He is certainly a most graceful man," she wrote. "He has a manner extremely polite and attentive."

It is no wonder that he had the pick of the belles at Mrs. James K. Polk's cotillions, and was forever extricating himself from lovers' quarrels. But there was talk of Houston as the logical successor to Jackson as president, and friends advised him to settle down to married life. Time enough for that, the thirty-five-year-old Houston told them.

What he did not tell them was that he was, for once, deeply in love. The girl he adored was blonde, blue-eyed Eliza Allen, eighteen-year-old daughter of John Allen, one of the wealthiest and most influential men of Sumner County. Their engagement was announced in December, 1828, and Andrew Jackson, friend of the Allens as well as of Houston, gave them his blessing before he left Nashville for the White House.

The wedding was at twilight, by candlelight, in the parlor of the Allens' big white home standing high above the Cumberland River three miles beyond Gallatin. Rev. William Hume, pastor of Nashville's fashionable First Presbyterian Church, performed the ceremony, and Middle Tennessee's top society crowded the festive scene that January 22, 1829.

The next day, under a graying sky, Eliza, eldest of seven children, waved good-bye to her little sisters and brothers and rode off on horseback beside her new husband for Nashville and the excitement of his second campaign for governor. But there was something pathetically bleak in the whole scene, and before the day was over the black sky spilled a snowstorm that stopped them in their tracks—prophetic, perhaps, of the sudden storm that would end their marriage and his political career in Tennessee in twelve short weeks.

Eliza Walks Out

The snow that fell on Gov. Sam Houston and his nineteen-year-old bride the day after their wedding was something stunned Tennesseans would remember months later. But only now is there authentic explanation of the bitterness that blanketed their icy horseback ride and shattered their marriage three months later.

The mystery of their separation, on the very day the thirty-five-year-old governor of Tennessee opened his campaign for his second term, exploded into headlines across the nation. Eliza Allen, the Gallatin beauty who had just passed her nineteenth birthday when she married Sam Houston, was suddenly the most mysterious woman in the nation. The wall of silence she built around herself from that day on, the matching silence of Houston, and the fact that she destroyed all correspondence and all portraits of herself before she died only intensified the mystery. In haunted years to come, in Texas cabins and Washington taverns, Houston would drink himself unconscious, but his tongue was never loose enough to discuss his revered Eliza.

The shock of coming home to their rooms at the Nashville Inn one night, after a triumphant campaign opening, to find his marriage with Eliza ended forever, stunned him into the most dramatic exit from Tennessee history on record. The staggering road he took from there to Texas fame, winning much of Mexico for our country, led him close to the presidency. But there was always the mystery about Eliza to cast doubts. Politicians manufactured their own absurd versions of what had so tragically ended the marriage, but there was an eyewitness who told about the way it had begun, in the snow.

Houston and his bride had set out for Nashville the morning after the wedding, but by mid-afternoon the blinding snowstorm stopped them. They were within six miles of Nashville's public square, but Houston decided to stay overnight at Locust Grove, the two-story log home of his friends Mr. and Mrs. Thomas Martin. Next morning, as Mrs. Martin stood at a window watching a snowball fight between her two young daughters and Governor Houston, Eliza came down the stairs.

"It seems as if General Houston is getting the worst of the snowballing," Mrs. Martin greeted Eliza. "You had better go out and help him."

To which, to Mrs. Martin's utter amazement, Eliza calmly answered: "I wish they would kill him. I wish from the bottom of my heart that they would kill him."

Mrs. Martin was Houston's friend, and she said nothing of this until after the separation. The governor and his bride lived quietly in Nashville, seeing few people, occasionally visiting relatives.

On March 18, less than two months after Eliza's wedding, her baby brother, ten-month-old Charles, died, and it is probable that Eliza returned home for the funeral. At any rate, there was sadness and homesickness for the beautiful riverside farm of her parents, for Eliza was left alone in her hotel room much of the time while her husband went about his business as governor, planning his campaign for reelection.

It was going to be a close race. William Carroll, who had already had two terms as governor, had a strong following. Both he and Houston were friends of President Andrew Jackson, the most powerful politician in the nation at that time. Nobody could be sure, at that moment, which candidate Jackson would back.

Saturday afternoon, April 11, was set as opening date for the campaign. Both men spoke at a rally at Cockrill Springs (now the Centennial Park site), where the militia paraded and passed in review, and Davidson County Sheriff Willoughby Williams, in charge of the review, circulated through the crowd to see what the reaction to the two candidates was.

Williams was jubilant at what he heard. There was no doubt that Houston would be elected. He could hardly wait to ride back toward Nashville with Houston and give him the good news. "It afforded much gratification," Williams reported. "I left him in fine spirits."

That was Saturday night, and the world had turned upside down, it seemed to Williams, by the time he rode into Nashville early the next Thursday morning to check in at the Nashville Inn.

"Have you heard the news?" the desk clerk whispered as Williams signed the register. "General Houston and his wife have separated and she has gone to her father's house."

Williams hurried to Houston's room and found him in deepest dejection. The only other person in the room was Dr. John Shelby, one of Nashville's finest physicians and wealthiest citizens. It was at Dr. Shelby's daughter's wedding two years before that Sam Houston had danced so gracefully with that South Carolina belle on her honeymoon. Dr. Shelby, from Sumner County, had known Eliza Allen and her family all his life. He was perhaps the one man best qualified to advise her and Houston.

Williams begged Houston to put an end to the rumors. Houston, haggard and silent, shook his head. The rumors were true, all right. He had nothing more to say.

When Williams crossed the street from the inn to his office in the courthouse, he could hardly get past the crowds pushing and shoving in the corridors, in the various offices, and in his own office. All the talk was about Houston and his wife of three months.

"Is it true?" they were asking. Had Eliza actually been in love with someone else before she married Houston? Had her family urged her to marry Houston because of his prominence as governor, former attorney general, probable successor to Jackson as president? Had Houston found her weeping over old love letters when he came home that night? Or had she already left for her father's home?

Or was the trouble with Houston? Divorce was almost unheard of then. Nothing short of crime could bring it on, most people thought. Who was to blame? Theories popped up thick and ugly. Nobody could really believe any evil of the forthright, reserved Eliza. The trouble had to be with Houston.

Williams rushed back to the inn to tell Houston the temper of the crowd. By that time the governor was bent over his desk, writing his letter of resignation. Williams had never seen Houston so shaken. He had known him since boyhood—had stood beside him in Maryville the day Houston joined the army, had met the sapling litter that bore the wounded Houston back from the battlefield to his mother's home. He knew Houston's black moods, but he had never seen him so completely defeated.

"I can make no explanation" was all Houston would say to any of Williams' entreaties. "I exonerate this lady freely, and I do not justify myself. I am a ruined man, will exile myself, and now ask you to take my resignation to the Secretary of State."

When Williams pleaded with Houston not to think of resigning, to consider what disaster it would bring to his political friends, the governor replied, "It is my fixed determination, and my enemies when I am gone will be too magnanimous to censure my friends."

Houston at length finished his first draft of the letter, addressed to the speaker of the state senate, who would succeed him until election day brought a new governor. "Executive Office, Nashville, Tennessee, April 16, 1829," he headed the letter dissolving "the political connection which has so long, and in such a variety of form, existed between the people of Tennessee and myself."

With masterful restraint, Houston revealed the pain, concealed the cause. "No private afflictions however deep or incurable," he said, "can forbid an expression of the grateful recollections so eminently due to the kind partialities of an indulgent public. In reviewing the past, I can only regret that my capacity for being useful was so unequal to the devotion of my heart."

"Overwhelmed by sudden calamities" as he was, Houston gallantly insisted that it was "by my own misfortunes more than by the fault or contrivance of anyone."

What misfortunes? He refused ever to breathe a word of it to anyone. Only now does the truth appear.

Neither did he bother to tell to what lengths he had gone to get Eliza to return to him, to reconsider the separation. He had followed her to Gallatin, had had two talks with her—the second granted by Eliza only if her aunt were present.

Years later the aunt described the scene: "He knelt before her and with tears streaming down his face implored forgiveness . . . and insisted with all his dramatic force that she return to Nashville with him. Had she yielded to these entreaties, what the future may have brought to them none can tell. As it was, there were many years of sadness to be endured."

Houston had written to Eliza's father, begging his help in bringing about a reconciliation and admitting that he had made false accusations. "If mortal man had dared to charge my wife or say aught against her virtue, I would have slain him," Houston wrote John Allen, and continued: "That I have and do love Eliza none can doubt and that I have ever treated her with affection she will admit; that she is the only earthly object dear to me God will bear witness. . . . Eliza stands acquitted by me. I have received her as a virtuous, chaste wife and as such I pray God I may ever regard her, and I trust I ever shall. She was cold to me, and I thought she did not love me; she owns that such was one cause of my unhappiness. You can think how unhappy I was united to a woman who did not love me. That time is now past, and my future happiness can only exist in the assurance that Eliza and myself can be more happy, and that your wife and yourself will forget the past, forget all and find lost peace. . . . Let me know what is to be done."

But Eliza, who always stood straight as a ramrod, said there was nothing to be done. When Houston mounted his horse and rode away down the hill, along the winding road to Nashville, he knew his last hope was gone.

Back in his room at the Nashville Inn, Houston wanted only to be alone. He knew how his political rivals had made hay of the private tragedy. He knew that enraged mobs in Gallatin had burned him in effigy and that the same thing was threatened in Nashville. People who had basked in his smile the week before suddenly disclaimed any friendship.

For a week following his resignation, Houston locked himself in his room, in an agony of self-blame, tortured by "moments which few have felt and I trust none may ever feel again," he said years later. He had never belonged to any church, but he sent for Rev. William Hume, the Presbyterian minister who had performed his marriage ceremony so recently. He asked the minister to baptize him, and Hume promised to take the matter up with Rev. Obadiah Jennings, also of First Presbyterian Church. "Mr. Jennings and myself . . . declined on good grounds, as we think, to comply with his wishes in relation to that ordinance," Dr. Hume said.

But there were a few true friends who supported Houston in his troubled hours, and they kept pleading with him to put an end to the gossip by explaining the trouble. Honor forbade. "This is a painful, but it is a private affair," Houston replied. "I do not recognize the right of the public to interfere in it, and I shall treat the public as if it had never happened. . . . Whatever may be said by the lady or her friends, it is no part of the conduct of a gallant or a generous man to take up arms against a woman. If my character cannot stand the shock, let me lose it."

On Thursday, April 23, just a week after his resignation, Houston, in disguise, left the Nashville Inn and walked down the steep slope of the street to the river to board the packet *Red Rover*. Sheriff Williams was on one side of Houston, Dr. Shelby on the other, and a small procession behind. Houston was on his way to Indian territory, to rejoin the Cherokee friends of his boyhood who now lived in Arkansas. He had turned his back on the white man and would seek the peace of the red man again.

But in that "darkest, direst hour of human misery," so many of Nashville's influential men were beginning to doubt Houston's guilt that blame was shifting in the other direction. Eliza's family was enraged. When the *Red Rover* reached Clarksville, two of the men in the Allen family boarded the boat and demanded that Houston make a written statement denying the rumors that he had been "goaded to madness and exile by detecting our sister in crime."

Houston refused to have a part in any such wrangle, but he asked his callers to "publish in the Nashville papers that if any wretch ever dares to utter a word against the purity of Mrs. Houston I will come back and write the libel in his heart's blood." Eliza's relatives left the boat and decided, for the present, not to give any more publicity to the affair.

Houston, pacing the deck that evening, grew more and more despondent over "the bitter disappointment I had caused General Jackson and all my friends, and especially the blight and ruin of a pure and innocent woman who had entrusted her whole happiness to me." In his "agony of despair," he was "strongly tempted to leap overboard and end my worthless life." But at that moment an eagle swooped low, almost touching Houston's head, then "soaring aloft, with wildest screams, was lost in the rays of the setting sun."

Houston—the poet, the mystic, the Indian-moody Raven of Cherokee land—saw something symbolic in it. He would not kill himself.

"I knew then," he said, "that a great destiny waited for me in the West."

But Eliza, terribly alone at her father's suddenly gloomy home, the center of the nation's prying speculation, heard no eagle's scream to destiny. She wanted nothing so much as oblivion. She wanted not even a tombstone to mark her grave when she died. She could not bring herself to discuss the matter with even her family at first, but old friends were loyal and protective.

Balie Peyton, a twenty-six-year-old Sumner County neighbor who was to find fame as racehorse breeder, diplomat, soldier, and congressman, was one of Eliza's oldest friends. On a visit to her home, he persuaded her to confide in him about what had broken up her marriage to the governor, who was also his friend. That conversation, recorded in a document kept in the Peyton family until recently, was made public for the first time in this story in the Nashville *Tennessean Magazine*.

"I reminded Eliza of our friendship of long standing, and I said to her, 'I cannot reconcile it to myself to believe that you could be fickle, and cruel to a noble man like Houston,'" Peyton said.

"I believe you are my true friend," Eliza answered, "and I will tell you everything, for I value your good opinion, but you must solemnly promise to keep secret what I say to you. . . ."

Eliza Tells of Her Nightmare Marriage

"I left General Houston because I found he was a demented man," Eliza Houston blurted out the secret at last. "I believe him to be crazy!"

It was a bombshell to Balie Peyton, her trusted friend, as they managed a private conversation at her father's home near Gallatin shortly after the separation rocked the state with ugly rumors. Houston had resigned as governor of Tennessee, had thrown away his chance at becoming president, had begun the tortuous path that would lead him to the presidency of Texas and national fame. In deep despair, Houston had fled Nashville and sought oblivion among the Cherokees in Arkansas.

Peyton, the "southern horseman supreme" who was to win distinction himself as war hero, congressman, United States minister to Chile, was a good friend of Houston's, too. "I was shocked, and urged Eliza to explain herself," Peyton said of this conversation.

Eliza, only nineteen years old at the time, stood her ground. "He is insanely jealous and suspicious," she said of the thirty-five-year-old Houston, her husband for three months. "He required of me to promise not to speak to anyone, and to lock myself in my room if he was absent, even for a few moments, and this when we were guests in my own aunt's home! On one occasion, he went away early to attend to affairs in the city of Nashville, and commanded me not to leave my room until his return. I indignantly refused to obey, and after he was gone, I found he had locked the door and carried off the key, leaving me a prisoner until late at night, without food, debarred from the society of my relatives, and as a prey to chagrin, mortification and hunger."

But that was not all. The dauntless military hero was

afraid of the dark, and was in touch with the "spirit world."
"He gave an additional evidence of an unsound mind by his
belief in ghosts," Eliza said. "He was timid and averse to
being alone at night, on account of these imaginary and
supernatural influences, though ready to cope with any sort
of foe in the flesh, in the daytime!"

Why had she married him? Eliza had known General
Houston since she was a child, when he first came to her
father's home to visit him and his two brothers, Robert and
Campbell Allen, fellow officers in the War of 1812. On his
trips to Washington when he was congressman, Houston had
stopped overnight with the hospitable Allens in their big
white house overlooking the Cumberland. During Gallatin's
racing season, the Allen home was headquarters for the
horsey set, including Andrew Jackson and Houston.

When Jackson left for the White House on January
18, 1829, he had "rejoiced" in the fact that his good
friend Houston would be married four days later to the
Allens' eldest daughter—"a beautiful young lady, of accomplished manners," Jackson said. Eliza, in turn, had been
charmed by Houston's glamour, his talk of distant and exotic
places.

"I should never have consented to marry him had I not
been attracted by his brilliant conversation and his handsome
and commanding presence," Eliza told Balie Peyton.

"I parted from General Houston because he evinced no
confidence in my integrity, and had no respect for my intelligence, or trust in my discretion. I could tell you many
incidents to prove this but I would not say or do anything
to injure him, and that is why I require you not to speak
of all this."

Balie Peyton kept his promise. He never breathed a
word of the conversation until all possibility of harming

Houston or Eliza was gone. Both had been dead for years before he was persuaded to tell.

Peyton himself was near death, in 1878, when a Nashville newspaper published a story speculating on the Houston divorce. Peyton's daughter, Emily, was indignant about the unfair speculation.

"Father, you must know all about this," Emily, a strong-minded woman who had been secretary to the American legation in Chile when her father was U.S. minister there, said. "Tell me: why did Mrs. Houston leave the General?"

"Yes, I do know," Peyton replied. "As the parties most interested are no longer living, I do not suppose there will be any objection to my relating the facts to you now."

What Balie Peyton told his daughter is revealed here for the first time. Emily wrote it in ink, on ruled legal paper. The first and last pages of the "letter" are missing, and it is possible that she meant it only as a written record. At any rate, her father began his recollection of the conversation with Eliza by making it clear that there was no romantic relationship between him and Eliza.

"Eliza was a person of the finest traits of character— modest, sensible and with a rare dignity of carriage," Peyton began. "No one could presume to take a liberty with her. I was her sincere friend, though never a lover. . . ."

When Peyton had finished his story of Houston's jealousy and cruelty to Eliza, Emily was furious. "Dignity and firmness," Emily wrote, "were Eliza's distinguishing characteristics." She had known Eliza in her later years, when she remarried, and remembered her as a "devoted wife" of a Gallatin physician, a "fond mother of her two daughters."

"It is true that Mrs. Houston did not belong to that class of persons who 'wear their hearts on their sleeves for daws to peck at,' " Emily Peyton wrote, "but she was capable of lasting and devoted affection for those whom she esteemed." What's more, Emily said, there was not a word of truth in the published theory that Eliza's family had encouraged her into a loveless marriage because of the prominence of Houston. On the contrary, Jo Conn Guild, a leading citizen in Sumner County, said it was to Houston's advantage socially to marry into the Allen family. "It is my privilege and my duty to prove that so far from being activated by coldness and caprice, Mrs. Houston had the best of reasons for her conduct," Emily Peyton wrote. "I am sure that at the time of her marriage, no intimation was given of undue influence, or coertion on the part of her parents. . . ."

"Where is the woman in our glorious, free country who would as a bride consent to be locked up by an exasperating Bluebeard, like a slave, or a criminal?"

Writing the account of her father's conversation with Eliza, Emily Peyton felt that she was helping Eliza, "after the lapse of more than sixty years, with her own hand, as it were, lift the curtain of the mystery that so enshrouded her in this life." But having written the seven-page document, Emily folded it and tucked it away with the family correspondence, where it lay in the attic of the Gallatin home of her nieces.

When the nieces, Miss Louise Peyton and her sister, the late Miss Mary Bugg Peyton, sold their home several years ago, out came the boxes of family letters, including Emily's account of her father's conversation with Eliza Houston. Only in the summer of 1962 did this reporter learn about the document from Miss Elizabeth Allen (great-niece of Eliza Allen) of Gallatin, and Miss Louise Peyton gave the *Tennessean Magazine* permission to publish it.

But Eliza did not tell all to Balie Peyton. She confided to certain members of her own family, and later to her

son-in-law, Dr. William D. Haggard, a more personal reason
for the separation. For the first time, members of the Allen
family and descendants of Dr. Haggard revealed that information for publication. Neither knew that the other knew
until they told the story, separately, to this reporter.

"My grandfather, Dr. Haggard [father of the late Dr. W.
D. Haggard of Nashville], was not only the confidant of his
mother-in-law, Eliza Houston Douglass," John Haggard of
Nashville said. "He was also at one time Houston's physician. He knew about the wound that the barbed arrow had
left in Houston. The opening into the intestine never healed,
and the intestinal discharge, through the wall of the ab-
domen, was an unpleasant thing for Houston, a revolting
thing for a sensitive woman like Eliza Allen."

Eliza told her family about the offensive "running sore"
in Houston's "groin." That, presumably, was "my own
misfortune" that Houston blamed for the separation in his
letter of resignation as governor.

It was, presumably, the "running sore" that made Eliza
"cold" to Houston, and it was the coldness that stirred
him to unreasonable jealousy. It was the combination of
the two that wrecked his marriage, and both reasons were
too personal to mention in public statements. In his rage
of jealousy, Houston had made accusations against Eliza he
would regret the rest of his life. As he pleaded for forgiveness,
she could think of nothing but the unpardonable insult.

So Houston cut himself off from Tennessee and the
tragic marriage forever. He sought his Cherokee friends in
Arkansas who had lived in Tennessee, near his Maryville
home, when he was a boy. There the old chief who had
once adopted him welcomed Houston back into the tribe,
and Houston plunged into the business of helping negotiate
peace with the Creeks, the Choctaws, and the Osages.

He knew the Indian mind. He overawed them with his commanding appearance, his flair for the dramatic, his unvarying loyalty. Eight weeks after he rejoined the Cherokees, he had ridden hundreds of miles to confer with many chiefs. He had become a great power in the West, "easily controlling all of the Indians from Missouri to Texas."

Though still married to Eliza, Houston took a Cherokee wife—according to their custom—the tall and lovely Tiana Rogers, sister of his best boyhood friends. (Tiana never had children, but one of her brothers was grandfather of the famous Will Rogers.) Houston built a log house for Tiana, set out an orchard for her, and found peace of a sort. But he could not get Eliza out of his mind. He drank heavily, ate little, rode horseback through the roughest weather on Indian missions to Saint Louis, all over the Oklahoma territory—"anything to re-create my mind," he said.

Eliza had returned her engagement ring to him, and Indians (with whom he never drank) would find him slouched under a tree in a driving rain, too drunk to stand, staring at a little leather pouch where he carried the ring. Some travelers through the territory said the new name the Indians gave him, Oo-tse-tee Ar-dee-tah-skee, meant "Big Drunk." Others said it meant "Super Man." Both applied.

The giant frame finally collapsed in a burning malarial fever, and for weeks the Indians who watched over Houston despaired of his life. But two years later he was on his way to Washington, heading a delegation of Indians. They passed through Nashville, and Houston took them on a tour of the Hermitage, home of his great friend, the president they were to see.

News of Houston's appearance in Tennessee touched off panic among the politicians. They had heard that Eliza Allen had changed her mind and wanted to go back to Houston.

If the two were reunited, Houston could become a formidable political power again. The politicians whipped up press releases that fanned the old fires of scandal, heaping insults on Houston that would surely ruin him forever, they thought.

Yet Houston remained silent. He said later that even if Eliza had come to him then, "I would not have received her." He had thrown away a career, almost his life, to forget her. There was no turning back. In Washington, when President Jackson and his niece, Mrs. Sarah Yorke Jackson, received him with great kindness, Houston showed his appreciation with a very special gift to her: Eliza's engagement ring.

As it turned out, the Indian business that had taken him to Washington was the least important thing that happened to him there. Soon after Houston arrived, Washington newspapers published a story about a speech William Stanbery, congressman from Ohio, had made in the House, implying that Houston had made fraudulent profit from his deals with the Indians. Houston stormed to the House foyer to "settle" the matter, and James K. Polk, then a congressman, hustled him outside to cool off. Houston sent Tennessee's Congressman Cave Johnson inside with a challenge to a duel to be presented to Stanbery, who refused to accept a challenge from a man he did not know.

"I'll introduce myself to the damned rascal," Houston said, and Stanbery armed himself with two pistols.

One night two weeks later, on April 13, 1832, Houston and several congressmen friends dropped by Tennessee Sen. Felix Grundy's hotel for a chat and then walked along dark Pennsylvania Avenue toward Houston's hotel. Suddenly crossing the street ahead of them, a man came into full sight under the streetlamp. One of Houston's companions recognized Congressman Stanbery and hurried away, while Houston blocked Stanbery's way.

"Are you Mr. Stanbery?" Houston asked.

"Yes, sir," the congressman answered.

"Then you are a damned rascal," Houston said as he whacked a hickory cane over Stanbery's head.

Stanbery was also a huge man, and the two were soon on the pavement, with Stanbery yelling for help. Stanbery pressed a pistol against Houston's chest and pulled the trigger, but it did not fire. Houston tore the gun from Stanbery's hand, stood up to give Stanbery more licks with the cane, and finished the performance by lifting the congressman's feet in the air and striking him "elsewhere," as a witness delicately put it.

The resulting furor occupied Congress and the nation's newspapers for the next month. Stanbery had Houston arrested for attacking him for remarks he had made on the floor of Congress, and the congressional investigation was the most sensational thing that had happened in Washington in years.

When Houston—handsome and mysterious in Indian-style buckskin coat—walked down the aisle of the House and bowed low before the Speaker, the galleries were packed for the performance. Day after day, for a month, other stories took whatever newspaper space was left after full coverage of the Houston trial. Francis Scott Key, author of "The Star-Spangled Banner," was Houston's lawyer, but Houston did most of his own defending. His argument—rather thin—was that it was not what Stanbery said in the House that made him accountable, but what he was quoted as saying in the papers.

Even President Jackson, Houston's staunch friend, felt that the decision would be against him. Houston was taken by surprise on May 6 when he was notified he would have to wind up his defense the next day. His approach to the crisis was typical. That night Houston—the man afraid to be alone in the dark—had plenty of company. Balie Peyton, the man to whom Eliza had confided her secret, was among the friends who came by Houston's room to cheer him. So were the Speaker of the House and Senator Grundy.

Some of the crowd, after many drinks, fell asleep on the couches, but all at length went home. Toward dawn, Houston—alone with his headache and his coffee—began to deck himself out in new finery bought for the occasion. When he appeared before the House that day, with every aisle packed, the stage was set for one of the most dramatic moments in his life.

With a composure that stunned even his opponents, Houston rose to an oratorical peak. His timing, his voice, and his rare histrionic ability had the greatest actor of the day, Junius Booth, rushing down the aisle to pay homage to Houston the minute the speech was over.

But it was not all acting. The logic was there. The inspiration was there. Calling on all defenders of personal freedom from the Apostle Paul to Blackstone, ringing in the perils of every tyrannical government from ancient Greece to Napoleon, Houston argued that his case was a test of every American citizen's heritage of freedom and the right to protect his own name. "When you shall have destroyed the pride of American character you will have destroyed the brightest jewel that heaven ever made," he concluded.

Houston got off with a mild reprimand. More important, he was a national figure again. He decided to seize the moment to carry out plans that had been in the back of his mind for four years: to help restless Texans win their territory from Mexico.

In 1832 he said farewell to Tiana, his Cherokee bride, and left her the house, the farm, and their two slaves. On

December 2, 1832, Houston entered Texas, the scene of his greatest triumphs. There, as commander in chief of Texas armies, he was to weld that disorganized force into a fine-edged tool to hack the crafty Santa Anna's Mexican forces down in defeat.

But it was a slow-going enterprise, with plots and counterplots to wrest the power from Houston. The man who Eliza had said was afraid of the dark "shut himself up in small taverns, seeing nobody by day and sitting up all night"—writing, planning, sometimes despairing.

When he was marching his forces toward the Alamo to rescue the Americans trapped there, he put his ear to the ground, Indian style, and knew the battle nearly a hundred miles away was over. The firing had ceased. News of the butchering of every last man at the Alamo so demoralized the army that, historians say, only the force of Houston's personality held it together. For forty-eight horrible hours—"the darkest in my life," Houston said—without food or sleep, he whipped his army into position for the big battle at San Jacinto.

For five days, in Indian silence—inscrutable, stony-faced—Houston refused to explain his tactics. His only sleep was for two hours at dawn. Through the night he would check the encampment, taking other officers along for company. In his tent, by candlelight, he would read *Julius Caesar* or *Gulliver's Travels*, or write letters.

On the day of the crucial battle, April 21, 1836, he awoke from a daybreak sleep to see an eagle circling the sky. It was an omen of victory for Houston.

That afternoon, as Houston gave the signal for the attack, the call "Remember the Alamo! Remember the Alamo!" electrified the ranks. In twenty ghastly minutes the battle was won. Houston, with about half the number of men the

Mexicans had, had accomplished a victory "unparalleled in the history of the world."

The Mexicans suffered 1,568 casualties: 630 killed; 208 wounded; 730 prisoners, including Santa Anna. Houston lost 26 men: 6 killed and 20 wounded. Houston himself had two horses shot from under him and fell off the third in a faint just as the battle ended. His right boot was full of blood, and his leg, shattered just above the ankle, was in agonizing pain.

But Texas was an independent republic now, and San Jacinto became password to all the glory the Republic of Texas, and later the State of Texas, could press on him: president of the republic, commander in chief of the armies, governor of the state, U.S. senator.

Back in Gallatin, Eliza Houston told friends she would never get a divorce. When Tennessee friends approached Houston to suggest a reconciliation, he told them it was impossible. He would never revive the hurts he had suffered so to forget.

Houston had been courting a Texas girl, Anna Raguet, the accomplished daughter of a prominent Texan. When word came that Tiana, his Indian "wife," had died in 1838, Houston got a divorce from Eliza and asked Anna to marry him. But Anna, miffed when she learned he was just getting a divorce, turned him down—to her regret soon afterward.

Houston had the bottle to help him forget. And on a trip to Washington in May, 1839, he stopped in Mobile to visit a friend. There, at a garden party, he met the gentle Margaret Lea, twenty-year-old daughter of a wealthy family from Marion, Alabama. Their marriage, at the beautiful Lea home near Marion on May 9, 1840, began the happiest venture of Houston's life. It had been eleven years since his marriage to Eliza Allen, and Houston was forty-seven years old now.

Just six months after Houston's marriage to Margaret
Lea, Eliza Allen was married to Dr. Elmore Douglass, in the
fall of 1840. For twenty-one years Eliza and Dr. Douglass
lived quietly on a shaded street near Gallatin's courthouse
square, and two of their four children lived to adulthood. It
was their oldest daughter, Martha Allen Douglass, who married Dr. W. D. Haggard, and Eliza discussed with him the old
battle wound of Houston's that had so repelled her. He knew
about it. He had seen it.

Eliza herself, "after a long and painful illness," the Allen
family Bible states, "departed this life on Sabbath Eve, March
3, 1861, aged 51 years, 3 months and 1 day." In that painful
illness, as she lay on her deathbed, Eliza commanded her
family to burn all her letters and portraits in the fireplace in
her bedroom, where she could see them go up in blazes. She
was determined to cut off every clue to the tragedy of her
marriage to Sam Houston. Even Eliza's second daughter,
Susie, when she died eight years later, was so determined
to follow the pattern of oblivion that she specified in her
will that "there shall be neither monument nor tombstone
at my grave." It is only in recent years that the Allen family
placed markers at the two graves in the shadowy Gallatin
Cemetery.

Meanwhile, Margaret Lea Houston had given a touch of
elegance to the governor's mansion when Houston became
Texas' first governor. She took her grand piano wherever they
moved, presided at the tea table with charm, and worked
hard to bring Houston into the Baptist church. At length,
after years of soul-searching, even that was accomplished.

Margaret, catering to every whim, kept their four homes
ready for occupancy whenever the mood to travel struck the
old soldier. With an hour's notice, she would have the children dressed (there were eight eventually), the trunks packed,

and the servants alongside them in the two carriages ready for their gay jaunts from Houston to Independence to Huntsville to Austin.

Houston, as senator from Texas, spent much time in Washington, too. There he risked his political career in an effort to prevent civil war, and his speech for preserving the Union became one of the classics of all oratory. But Texas would have none of it, and called Houston home. Yet in 1859 he was elected governor of Texas again, and in 1860 both Democrats and Republicans so admired his courageous stand that they discussed running him for the presidency.

But when Texas voted for secession, Houston was replaced as governor. In his farewell letter, the man who had done most to create the state wrote that "the severest pang is that the blow comes in the name of the state of Texas." His own son joined the Confederate army and was severely wounded at Shiloh. Houston was immensely proud of the youth's heroic conduct.

By 1862 Texans were begging Houston, "still a powerful figure at 69," to run again for governor, but he took a sudden cold in June, 1863, and died of pneumonia, murmuring, "Texas, Texas, Margaret," as Margaret bent over him. And Texas, which could not have evolved as it did if Eliza had not left him, has raised towering monuments to echo Houston's name forever.

Aaron Burr Was Framed

How a political campaign can ruin a man's life, can hound him across the world and far beyond the grave, is nowhere more strikingly illustrated than in the tragic career of Aaron Burr, the vice-president who missed being president of the United States by one vote.

Nashville was drawn into that national and international turmoil twice—once in 1805 and 1806 when Burr acted out some of the crucial hours of his stormy life in Nashville, and again twenty-two years later when Andrew Jackson ran for president and his political enemies accused him of having aided the "traitor" Burr.

Historians are just now digging up the records that indicate how unjustly Burr was accused of treason and show that he was a victim of "frame-ups." In 1807 the Supreme Court acquitted him, but Burr still stands condemned by political gossips and by textbooks that have perpetuated the tales that circulated as part of a bitter political contest.

Court papers in the possession of Spain, recently made available to historians, show that Burr was actually the victim of an American spy—"Number 13"—in the pay of Spain for almost two decades. That spy was the ear of President Thomas Jefferson, and through him turned all American officialdom in blinding wrath against Burr.

Documents in the possession of Nashville historian

Stanley Horn not only testify to the innocence of Burr's colonization plans—later branded as a form of treason—but also indicate the jealous fury of Thomas Jefferson at a man who had almost won the presidency from him. For Jefferson, author of our Constitution and champion of many of the beliefs held dearest by Americans, had an overpowering weakness: an intense jealousy of men who rivaled his leadership of his party.

Aaron Burr, descended from a family of college presidents, ministers, and scholars who had had a substantial part in shaping New England's development since the early 1600s, was a brilliant man, impatient with plodders. He was more intent on getting a thing done right than on pleasing his superiors.

That trait did not endear him to superior officers, including Gen. George Washington, when Burr fought during the Revolutionary War. Burr was only nineteen years old when he volunteered for some of the most dangerous campaigns of that war. By studying strategy at night and fighting by day, he was able to outwit the enemy on numerous telling occasions. Intent on saving soldiers' lives even as he gained victories, young Major Burr became an immediate hero to the men who served under him.

When he was transferred to General Washington's headquarters, on the outskirts of New York, Burr found the old general a slow thinker, a bungling strategist. When General Washington became president, he did not forget that the upstart Major Burr had dared correct his strategy, had countermanded the general's orders and given conflicting orders in an effort to save lives and win battles.

Washington stored that up against Burr. In later years, when Burr was proposed as ambassador to France, Washington vetoed the order. Still later, when black rumors about

Burr were whispered across the fledgling country, politicians said, "Washington never trusted him."

Even Alexander Hamilton, another young officer who was soon to serve under General Washington at his Richmond Hill headquarters, found the general a trial to work with. But Hamilton, long a close associate of Burr's and finally such a bitter enemy that they fought it out in a duel, always made a point of pleasing those in authority.

Hamilton had heavy odds against him. Born in the West Indies, the son of a French mother and a Scotch father who were never married, Hamilton had suffered deprivation and humiliation in his childhood. Through his own brilliant achievements as a boy and his own determination to get an education, he had aroused the sympathy of some West Indians, who raised money to send him to America.

He was fifteen years old when he arrived alone at Elizabethtown, New Jersey, studying for entrance to what is now Columbia University. That same year, at Princeton, New Jersey, sixteen-year-old Aaron Burr was graduating from the university where his father and his grandfather Jonathan Edwards had been president.

So evenly matched in brilliance, age, slight stature, fastidious appearance, social grace, professional ability, and military achievement, Hamilton and Burr had the same weaknesses: they were both always hopelessly in debt, making handsome fees as lawyers but living too lavishly to keep the bills paid. They were also constantly involved in love affairs, some of them of a scandalous nature.

Despite the fact that they practiced law together, often defended each other in litigation over debts, and were closely associated in general, Hamilton was ever the newcomer, the illegitimate son fighting hard to make a name for himself. Burr was born into a position of such authority and culture that it never occurred to him to "climb" or even to defend himself from those who would climb at his expense.

When three-year-old Aaron Burr and his little sister were left orphans, bereft of parents and grandparents within a year, their uncle Timothy Edwards took them in. He was so stern that Aaron ran away from home for four days when he was four years old. "He beat me like a sack," Burr recalled. When Aaron was ten years old, he ran away a second time, this time to sea. But at the end of his first voyage he was hauled out of the riggings where he hid and was forced to go home with his uncle.

Brought up in the tradition of the classics, as his ancestors had been, young Aaron had careful training from tutors and was ready to enter Princeton University when he was eleven years old. But the university turned him down because of his extreme youth, and Aaron, ready for the junior class when he was thirteen years old, had to content himself with being admitted as a sophomore.

Friends and relatives had assumed that he would go into the ministry, in the family tradition, and Aaron assumed that, too. But after his graduation from Princeton, he studied for the ministry for a few months and decided against it. Irritated at the limitations of any one church, he believed that "the road to Heaven is open to all alike."

From there he turned to law, and had hardly begun his law study when the Revolution began. Immediately he volunteered, and by the end of the war he had proved himself a military genius. He was a colonel at the age of twenty-two.

At the end of the war he was a melancholy young man, confused about his plans. He had fallen in love with a British officer's American widow, Mrs. Theodosia Prevost, and she advised him to take up the study of law again. Though three years' study was required before a student was eligible for the bar examination, an exception was made in his case—in view of his four years of military service. After three months' study, Burr passed the examination, and began his practice in Albany in 1782, when he was twenty-six.

That same year he was married to Mrs. Prevost, who had five children of her own and was ten years older than Burr. Not a particularly pretty woman, the widow was the descendant of generations of New England and Virginia scholars and ministers. Her brilliant mind and scholarly achievements matched Burr's.

But he lost her stabilizing influence only twelve years after their marriage. When she died of cancer, she left their eleven-year-old daughter, Theodosia, as Burr's one mainstay in the turbulent world that boiled about him. Burr was thirty-eight then, and was to remain a widower for thirty-nine years. His love affairs with prominent beauties of New York, Philadelphia, Washington, and half the capitals of Europe became legendary, but they never shut out of his mind his devotion to his brilliant and charming daughter.

The Richmond Hill mansion where he had first known George Washington became Burr's home, in addition to an impressive townhouse in New York. Tutors in French, Latin, Greek, and philosophy trooped in and out of the doors to train young Theodosia, and her father, in the state legislature in Albany or in the United States Senate at Washington, wrote her constantly to supervise her study.

"She reads so much and so rapidly that it is not easy to find proper and amusing French books for her," he wrote of Theodosia when she was nine. And when she was eleven, he was writing, "My dear little girl . . . I am sure you will be charmed with the Greek language above all others." Determined to bring up his daughter to prove that women could have brains, that they could achieve a state above the usual level of simpering, coquettish belles, he developed her into a dazzling young lady.

As official hostess at Burr's home, Theodosia helped entertain officialdom of many lands. When she was seventeen, she married Joseph Alston, a wealthy South Carolina planter who was later to become governor of that state. But even as her father's tragedy brought heartbreak to her, she wrote, "I had rather not live than not be the daughter of such a man."

Two years after he began his law practice, Burr was elected to the New York state legislature. Five years later he was appointed attorney general of the state. Two years after that, he was elected to the United States Senate. That was the beginning of his trouble with Hamilton. For Burr defeated Hamilton's father-in-law in that Senate race of 1791. Hamilton had married into one of New York's most prominent families, and he did not take lightly the defeat of his wife's father. Hamilton himself, through his carefully cultivated friendship with President Washington, had become secretary of the treasury when the government was set up. From the time Burr took the Senate seat out of the family until they met at pistol point thirteen years later, Hamilton, though outwardly friendly, never lost an opportunity to imply evil motives for Burr's every act.

By 1800 Burr had risen to such political heights that he ran on the ticket with Thomas Jefferson for the presidency. Jefferson, who had already served as vice-president and was recognized as head of the Republican (now Democratic) party, would be president and Burr would be vice-president. Yet, as the law then stood, the man who got the most electoral votes was president and the runnerup was vice-president.

Burr and Jefferson got an equal number of votes, and the election had to be settled in the House of Representatives.

There the congressmen were deadlocked for a week, through thirty-six ballots. Jefferson was in Washington, directing the activities of his followers, who worked feverishly to win votes. Burr remained in New York, feeling it improper to take part in the congressional deadlock either directly or indirectly. All the lobbying in Burr's favor was done by friends who worked without his direction or even cooperation.

"Had Burr done anything for himself, he would long ere this have been president," one of his friends in Congress wrote. "If a majority would answer, he would have it on every vote."

But Jefferson made "certain promises . . . in case he was elected," and in return "the opposition of Vermont, Delaware and Maryland was withdrawn. . . . That terminated the memorable contest." With those votes changed, the deal was made and Jefferson won the vote from Burr, who might have had it by bestirring himself for one vote. Members of both parties were so impressed by the dignity and conduct of young Burr—thirteen years younger than Jefferson—that they settled on him for the presidency in the next election: 1804.

Burr was so highly regarded by the opposition as well as by his own party that Jefferson and Hamilton saw in him a formidable opponent. Opposing each other bitterly, Jefferson and Hamilton, by coincidence, had this hate in common, and they worked along parallel lines on one project—to undermine Burr's reputation, to insinuate that he was not trustworthy and was no fit man for the presidency.

It was an age of pamphleteering, when unsigned attacks on public figures were regularly printed and distributed throughout the colonies. In a way, they were a form of communication in regions too far removed from the cities to have newspaper service, but they stooped to tactics so irresponsible that Burr never felt them worthy of his answer. Hamilton made the most of pamphleteer tactics.

So effective were the attacks against Burr in those years of his vice-presidency that by 1804, when he was to have been swept into the presidency by almost unanimous agreement, he was not even mentioned for the vice-presidency. Realizing at last that people did believe the pamphlets, he seized upon a clipping that a friend showed him. It quoted Hamilton as saying that Burr was "not to be trusted," and Burr wrote Hamilton for an explanation. The man who had so long written sly insults against Burr and had gone unchallenged began to wheedle and cringe, to pretend that he knew nothing about the statement.

But Burr pressed him for an explanation, and Hamilton— his own political future at stake if he had to admit that his attacks on Burr were not true—continued to refuse any explanation. Burr, according to the practices of the day, could only challenge Hamilton to a duel. Hamilton felt he would be disgraced if he did not accept the challenge, but he made it clear that he did not want to fight. His own son had been killed in a duel a few years before, and Hamilton said that he had religious convictions against the practice. Yet he would not apologize to Burr.

Dueling was already outlawed in New York, so the two men met just across the state line, in New Jersey, early on Wednesday morning, July 11, 1804. Witnesses have testified that all was in order, that every rule was observed. Hamilton had every advantage—he won the privilege of choosing position and shooting first. But Burr's bullet hit its target, and Hamilton's did not. From that hour, Burr was called "murderer."

As politicians exploited the affair and newspapers editorialized about it, public wrath grew so great that Burr found it wise to flee to the South. In his island refuge off the coast of Georgia in September, 1804, he narrowly missed death in one of the fiercest hurricanes that ever whipped the Atlantic coast. Negro servants on the plantation where he was guest were drowned and crushed to death by the scores in the storm that Burr described vividly in letters to Theodosia, and other dangers threatened him.

But he remained there until time for the Senate to convene in January, 1805. In those closing weeks of the Senate, he, as vice-president, presided over the body with such dignity and restraint that the senators were moved to tears when he made his farewell speech.

Fastidious in conduct as in appearance, he had schooled the senators in proper behavior on the Senate floor. He had stopped their backwoods custom of wandering about the Senate floor with apples and cheese in hand. He was embarrassed when Jefferson received the French ambassador in dirty corduroy knee breeches and coarse black stockings. He had built up a feeling of respect for the senators' office and for their responsibility in government.

"This house is a sanctuary, a citadel of the law, of order and of liberty," Burr told the senators in his farewell address. "And it is here . . . resistance will be made to the storms of political frenzy and the silent arts of corruption; and if the Constitution be destined ever to perish by the sacrilegious hands of the demagogue or the usurper—its expiring agonies will be witnessed on this floor."

At the end of his speech, without bitterness Burr bowed, "descended from the chair, and in a dignified manner walked to the door, which resounded as he with some force shut it after him," one senator described the ending of Burr's political life.

As the resounding door echoed on their silence, the

senators sat stunned by what he had said in those memorable "twenty or thirty minutes." He had spoken with "so much tenderness, knowledge and concern that it wrought upon the sympathy of the senators in a very uncommon manner. There was a solemn and silent weeping for perhaps five minutes. My colleague, General Smith, stout and manly as he is, wept as profusely as I did," the senator wrote. "He laid his head upon his table and did not recover from his emotion for a quarter of an hour or more. And for myself, though it is more than three hours since Burr went away, I have scarcely recovered my habitual calmness. . . . He is a most uncommon man."

Burr in Nashville

When Aaron Burr, the vice-president who missed being president of the United States by one vote, made his farewell speech to the Senate on March 2, 1805, he was a doomed man. He left the senators in stunned silence as he closed the door firmly and hurried down the corridors and out into a world suddenly empty and hostile. The senators wept, but there was nobody around to see whether the stoic Burr shed a tear.

Already called a murderer because he had killed Alexander Hamilton in a duel, he had, through his own brilliance and uncompromising nature, accumulated enough enmity to ruin his political prospects. But he had no inkling that jealous opponents would hound him to the grave and brand him in history as "traitor."

"Burr is one of the best presiding officers that ever presided over a deliberative body," one of the senators wrote that March afternoon of his valedictory. "Where he is going or how he is to get through with his difficulties I know not."

Where to turn next was indeed the question with the

forty-nine-year-old ex-vice-president. His New York property had been sold to pay his debts, and his daughter was married and settled in South Carolina. So like other men seeking a new life, he turned his thoughts westward.

Jefferson had just purchased the Louisiana territory, though through a strange error he had left Florida to Spain. Spain held the territory where Texas is now, as part of Mexico, and Hamilton, with other government leaders, had failed in a vast plot to take over much of Mexico and South America from the Spaniards. It occurred to Burr that he might succeed where others had failed, and he went west in pursuit of the plan.

Burr's scheme was to raise money by private subscription to purchase "one million acres of land" in Louisiana and to interest enterprising young men in going there to colonize the territory. He, like Jefferson and other political leaders of the day, was sure that the United States would soon be at war with Spain, and he felt that the Louisiana colony would make a good point of attack on Mexico. The United States was expanding rapidly, grabbing off land by purchase and by conquest, and Burr planned to be strategically located for the advance westward.

It was in the course of preparations for that expedition that Burr first went to Nashville. He had probably known Andrew Jackson in Congress, and it was said that Burr had been urged to settle in Nashville, resume his law practice there, get himself elected to Congress, and become Speaker of the House. But Burr had larger schemes in mind.

Jackson, who still lived in a log cabin on the Hermitage grounds, had not won national fame then, but he was a successful lawyer, planter, owner of a general store and boat-building business, and general of the state militia. It was as boat builder that he was sought out by Burr.

"Arrived at Nashville on the 29th of May," Burr wrote his daughter, Theodosia, in 1805. "One is astonished at the number of sensible, well informed and well behaved people which is found here. I have been received with much hospitality and kindness, and could stay a month with pleasure; but General Andrew Jackson having provided us a boat, we shall set off on Sunday, the 2nd of June, to navigate down the Cumberland . . . and on down the Mississippi to Natchez and New Orleans."

As guest of Jackson at the Hermitage, Burr had been much entertained, honored with "the most magnificent parades that had ever been made" in Nashville, and he was guest of honor at so many banquets that "everybody seemed to be contending for the honor of having best treated or served Colonel Burr."

In the boat that Jackson had lent him, he made part of the trip southward for further preparations for the expedition west. On August 6, 1805, he was back in Nashville, again much entertained during the ten days he was guest at the Hermitage. "The hospitality of these people will keep me here till the 12th instant, when I shall partake of a public dinner, given not to the vice-president, but to A. Burr," he wrote his daughter in some triumph.

A few days later he added: "For a week I have been lounging at the house of General Jackson, once a lawyer, after a judge, now a planter; a man of intelligence, and one of those prompt, frank, ardent souls whom I love to meet. The general has no children, but two lovely nieces made a visit of some days, contributed greatly to my amusement, and have cured me of all the evils of my wilderness jaunt. If I had time, I would describe to you these two girls, for they deserve it."

A Nashville observer wrote: "The invasion of Mexico was in every heart, on every tongue. All that was yet lacking to make it certain was war between Spain and the United States, and every Western or Southern man believed that war was at hand."

Burr's great weakness, Jackson observed, was that he trusted all men. Certainly his downfall was in trusting "General" James Wilkinson, a slippery Revolutionary War soldier who had first known Burr when they fought in the Quebec campaign. He had become Burr's confidant and right-hand man in all the preparations for the Louisiana colony and the subsequent invasion of Mexico.

What Burr could not know was that Wilkinson had been in the pay of Spain for eighteen years as a secret agent known as "Number 13." The original colonies, loosely strung together and not necessarily planning to stick together, were in a turmoil of hope and suspicion, attractive prey for various countries, and Wilkinson planned to be on the winning side— whichever it was.

Tennessee and Kentucky, with the Mississippi River as their only outlet to the world's markets, had strong commercial ties with the Spaniards, who controlled the country's southern coast. What went on in these "backwoods states" was always a matter of some suspicion to the easterners, and it was easy for them to believe the wildest rumors.

Jefferson himself foresaw an eventual splitting up of the various regions of the country, and he gave it his blessings. "If they see their interests in separation, why should we take sides with our Atlantic rather than our Mississippi descendants?" President Jefferson asked in 1803. "God bless them both, and keep them in union if it be for their good. But separate them if it be better."

Jefferson knew of Burr's plans for westward colonization and eventual attack on Spain, but it was wise, in the interest of peace with Spain, to say nothing of it. But when

Wilkinson, Spain's agent "Number 13," failed to collect his fee for revealing Burr's whole scheme to Spain, he turned to Jefferson with the information of Burr's "infamous plot."

"Cheated" of the more than one hundred thousand dollars that he had expected as pay from Spain for his spy services, Wilkinson was determined to make something off his information. He would at least appear a hero to Jefferson and the public.

It took little twisting of the tale to pretend that Burr not only meant to claim the territory that is now Texas for the United States, but actually would set up his own government there in opposition to the United States. Burr would march vast armies against Washington and overthrow the government, Wilkinson said.

Jefferson, still bitter toward Burr, the man who had barely missed taking the presidency away from him, never quite knew what to make of the scholarly little man who kept his peace, who went about his business quietly and almost mysteriously. "Jefferson will run like a cotton-tail rabbit," Jackson had told Burr when they first discussed the schemes. If word of the plans leaked out before the striking hour, Jefferson would deny any knowledge of it. He did.

So did Wilkinson. As he carefully planted the wildest rumors of treason and rebellion throughout the South and the West, he wrote Jefferson that he had only recently come into this gold mine of information. It was shocking to him, he said.

It was awkward for Jefferson, too. The long-expected war against Spain had been averted through a recent agreement, and all the good work might be undone if Jefferson admitted that the plan had his sanction all the time. But Jefferson might have put a stop to the rumors that Wilkinson had started, if he had chosen. Instead, by his silence at least, and by his air of indignation, Jefferson let the rumors blossom and multiply into such monstrous tales that even their author, Wilkinson, was impressed.

As late as October, 1806, when Burr arrived in Nashville again for a few days to purchase supplies for the expedition, he was still trusted there. "Dinner was given for Burr at Talbot's hotel on Saturday, October 28, the day he arrived in the city," Gen. John Coffee, prominent Nashville citizen, wrote. "Many of the most respectable citizens of Nashville and vicinity attended, drank toasts, gave suitable songs."

Dr. Felix Robertson, twice mayor of Nashville, and Jackson had, according to Burr's suggestion, made out a list of "enterprising young men" who might be interested in joining the colonizing expedition, and Jackson recommended his wife's nephew, Stockley D. Hays. Jackson, as general of the state militia, also promised Tennessee troops to help the expedition in case of war against Spain.

But by December, 1806, when Burr returned to Nashville for the last time, he saw the effects of the whispering campaign against him. Jackson was not at home, and Mrs. Jackson, who had always been hospitality itself toward Burr, gave him a cool reception. He was not invited in, so he went to the tavern at Clover Bottom, near the boat-building works.

The recently feted hero was shunned by all of Nashville, and he was a bitter, sharp-tongued man as he went about his business of outfitting barges and other boats for the expedition. John Coffee, who was a partner with Jackson and had charge of the boat-building phase of their joint operation, had been busy making "five flat boats and one keel boat" for Burr, having been paid $3,005 as a first installment and $50 later. Coffee watched Burr carefully as he rushed about in utter loneliness, and even quizzed him about the rumors.

"He was met coolly by those who before had acted

differently toward him," Coffee wrote. "At the Clover Bottom, nine miles from Nashville, where I then did business, there was a tavern, and to this place Colonel Burr came out and remained about a week, until he had gotten everything in readiness for his departure down the river."

Before the week was over, Jackson returned to Nashville, and he and Gen. Thomas Overton decided it was time they call on Burr and establish the truth about his purposes. Jackson had lost political strength himself by killing Charles Dickinson in a duel that same year, and he was perhaps doubly sensitive about being allied with Burr, the man banished from politics because he had killed Hamilton in a duel.

Burr assured them that "his views and objects were friendly to the government, that he had no views inimical to the government, none but what were known to the government and viewed with complaisance," and, a friend reported, "as well as my memory serves me, he showed them a commission in blank, with Mr. Jefferson's signature on it. . . ."

But even as Burr gave an account of his activities to Jackson, the orders for the arrest of the "traitor" were on their way. The fury of the rumors had gained such momentum that few dared stand by Burr. Wilkinson rushed about the South and the West, assuming authority to arrest members of Burr's party, having property of some of the colonizers destroyed, and putting New Orleans under military government while he took control of the city.

The other members of the party were at length released. Some of them sued the government for false arrest, and collected damages. But Jefferson had to save face. Because he and Wilkinson had to give their rumors some substantiation, they brought Burr to trial before the Supreme Court, sitting in Richmond.

John Marshall, chief justice of the Supreme Court, knew that Jefferson was so intent on convicting Burr that a failure to convict would endanger Marshall's whole career. He was aware of the vindictiveness of Jefferson, who had had judges impeached when they opposed him, but Marshall said in effect that Jefferson had not a leg to stand on when he brought the charges against Burr. He had Jefferson subpoenaed, so that he might be questioned on his previous knowledge of the scheme, but Jefferson refused. Jefferson, who had helped write the Constitution, stood in contempt of court.

All through the spring of 1807 Burr was held prisoner, and in the sweltering summer months the former vice-president was held in the Richmond jail, awaiting trial. "The most indefatigable industry is used by the agents of government, and they have money without stint," he wrote of Jefferson's attempts to gather evidence against him. "If I were possessed of the same means, I could not only foil the prosecutors, but render them ridiculous and infamous. The Democratic papers teem with abuse against me and my counsel, and even against the chief justice. Nothing is left undone or unsaid which can tend to prejudice the public mind, and produce a conviction without evidence."

In Nashville, at least one of those federal agents was busy trying to gather evidence against Burr. Sometimes he attended parties incognito and often mingled in crowds, trying to gain the confidence of people who might tell him something of Burr's activities in Nashville. "There was no evidence of treason in any conversation, private or otherwise," the federal agent had to report. "I could find nothing whatever to arouse any suspicion."

Andrew Jackson was called to Richmond to testify against Burr, but he made it known that his testimony would be in the other direction. That was embarrassing to the government, and it was infuriating to Jackson, after he had made the long trip to Richmond, to be denied the privilege of testifying. So Jackson took his message to the crowds in front of the Richmond courthouse, speaking forcefully on Burr's innocence and Jefferson's base "political persecution."

When the long summer's trial was over and Burr had been acquitted, there were banquets in his honor and speeches in his praise. But the crowds had had their appetites whetted for a victim, and they felt cheated. Burr's only way to safety, at least for the moment, seemed to lie in flight to Europe.

In England, Burr was entertained by leading writers and officials, but suddenly he was ordered out of the country, because Jefferson's representatives of our government in England had made it clear that the United States did not want Burr given haven. The U.S. government requested that Burr be deported from England.

It was a bitter blow, for Burr had been making a pleasant enough life for himself there. Now he found the trek was just beginning. He was shunned by first one country and then another, spending some time in Sweden, Denmark, Germany, and at length in France.

The funds that his debtors in America were supposed to have sent him never arrived. The letters that his daughter kept writing were seldom delivered, leaving him sometimes more than two years without word from home. Letters that he wrote her were intercepted. The packages that she sent him by friends going to Europe could no longer be delivered, for the friends had been warned by U.S. government officials to have nothing to do with him. The name "Burr" became a slander, and officials of other governments whom he had formerly entertained in his New York mansion had to turn a deaf ear to him; they had their orders from our government.

Living in cold garrets, hoarding a lump of coal for a grimy grate or a lump of sugar for a chilly cup of coffee, borrowing a few pennies—pennies he knew he could never repay—Burr suffered unspeakable humiliation and deprivation for four years of exile. And when he had determined to return to America and face his opponents openly, no matter what the consequences, the embassy denied him a passport. Ship captains were afraid to take him on board as a passenger. At length, after many delays, under an assumed name he did obtain a passport and passage to America. That was the course his daughter, Theodosia, had advised, though he never got her letters.

He hid in alleys and spent his first night in America in a shelter for vagrants, lying on a cot in a garret with five other men. The first word he had from his daughter after his return was a letter saying that her son, his only grandchild, had died. Her great dream was to see her father again and to help him get a new grip on life, and ill though she was, the twenty-nine-year-old Theodosia Burr Alston sailed from South Carolina for New York on the next to the last day of 1812.

Whether the ship went down in a storm off the coast of North Carolina, at treacherous Cape Hatteras, or whether pirates overtook the ship has never been known. In any case, neither the ship nor Theodosia was ever heard from again.

Aaron Burr's grief was complete. At fifty-six he was shorn of his last grip on the world. "I am severed from the human race," Burr wrote to his son-in-law, then governor of South Carolina.

But Burr had twenty-four more patient years to live out, in obscurity and contempt and hard work. He had a steady law practice, but he was never able to pay off his enormous debts. At seventy-seven he made a foolish marriage to a rich but inferior old lady, and in a few months the marriage was dissolved.

Three years later, on September 14, 1836, he died of the effects of a stroke. Funeral services were in the Princeton University chapel, and he was buried there—ironically enough—with full military honors, at the feet of his father and grandfather, former presidents of Princeton.

"You have read . . . that such things happen in all democratic governments," he had written his daughter in the midst of his trial for treason. "Was there in Greece or Rome a man of virtue and independence, and supposed to possess great talents, who was not the object of vindictive and unrelenting persecution?"

So vindictive were his enemies that it was not considered wise to put a marker at his grave. Twenty years after his death a stone was erected, but even now textbooks repeat the charges of his enemies, the charge that the United States Supreme Court acquitted him of: Treason.

Lincoya,
Old Andy's Little Indian

Nobody said for sure that the chubby Indian boy was crying when they found his parents dead on the battlefield. But when one of Andrew Jackson's officers found the child and asked surviving Indians who would take care of him, they all refused.

"Kill him too," the Indian women said sullenly. "You have killed the others."

Thus began the story of one of the most exotic members of Andrew Jackson's hospitable household. Lincoya, the year-old Indian boy, was taken home to the Hermitage to grow up as Jackson's son.

Time of the battle was November 3, 1813. Place was Creek Indian territory, in the lowest bend of the Tennessee River, near what is now Guntersville, Alabama. The fierce fight had boiled up out of outrage over the slaughter of 250 white people on August 30, 1813, when Creek Indians attacked Fort Mims, near Huntsville.

When word of the massacre came to Gen. Andrew Jackson, he was ill, in bed at the Hermitage, recovering from wounds suffered in a gun battle in an inn on Nashville's public square. His left shoulder had been so shattered that he almost bled to death and doctors told him they would have to amputate the arm.

"I'll keep the arm," Jackson had said firmly, and he was slowly gaining strength.

When he was asked to take command of an army to crush the Creek Indian uprising, Jackson began drawing up plans. He would have the troops mobilized and would take command at Fayetteville early in October.

He did, on October 7, with his arm in a sling and some of his men surly and indifferent about the campaign. They knew they were up against a fierce Indian chief, thirty-one-year-old "Red Eagle." Red Eagle, only one-eighth Creek, was actually the son and grandson of distinguished French, Scottish, and British forebears, and his real name was Willie Weatherford. His deep grudges against American settlers gave him special joy in butchering them.

But Jackson knew Indian warfare. When the battle was over, his men had killed every red warrior except Red Eagle (who surrendered later), and had captured eighty-four women and children huddled at Fort Deposit, near Huntsville.

"We shot them like dogs," Davy Crockett, one of Jackson's soldiers, reported.

It was a young officer who spotted little Lincoya, the Indian baby whose parents had both been slain. Still a nursing baby, he was hungry. When the Indian women refused to care for him, the officer brought the child to his commanding officer. There, against the bloody backdrop of frontier revenge, occurred one of the remarkable scenes of Jackson's life. With his left arm still in a sling, he reached down to feed the orphaned "savage."

Jackson himself had been orphaned by the Revolutionary War. And at that very moment he had in his home, at the Hermitage, a three-year-old nephew whom he had adopted and given his name, Andrew Jackson, Jr.

There was no milk on the battlefield, but Jackson ordered one of his men to bring some brown sugar and dissolve it in water. "With his one good hand, General Jackson coaxed the child to drink it," another officer reported. "Then he sent him to Huntsville to be looked after at his personal expense."

Meantime, on December 14, 1813, Jackson wrote his wife, Rachel, about the Indian child that he was going to send to the Hermitage as playmate for their adopted son: "I have instructed Major White to carry to you the little Lincoya. He is the only branch of his family left, and the others, when offered to them to take care of, would have nothing to do with him, but wanted him to be killed. . . . Quals, my interpreter, carried him on his back and brought him to me. Charity and christianity says he ought to be taken care of and I send him to my little Andrew and I hope will adopt him as one of our family."

On March 4, 1814, Jackson was still trying to arrange for someone to take the Indian baby to the Hermitage. "To amuse Andrew and to make him forget his loss, I have asked Col. Hays to carry Lyncoya to him," Jackson wrote Rachel from Fort Strother.

Rachel replied three weeks later: "Dear Andrew talks very much of his Little Lyncoia. . . . I am vexed that none of our friends will Fetch him to me." Two weeks later the Indian child had arrived at the Hermitage, and was wrapped in Rachel's devotion. "Your little Andrew is well," she wrote Jackson on April 7, 1814. "He is much pleased with his Charley. I think him a fine boy indeed."

Jackson began referring to the child regularly as his son. "Kiss my two sons and accept my prayers for your health and happiness until I return," he wrote Rachel from Florida in April, 1818.

In 1821, when Jackson was back at the Hermitage, settled for a time from his public duties, he wrote of his plans for educating the two boys. "I have my little sons, including

Lincoyer, at school, and their education has been greatly neglected in my absence," he wrote a friend in May, 1822, when the Indian child was about ten years old.

There were stories about the way the boy was showing his savage ancestry. He decorated his head with turkey feathers, and with a bow and arrow he made for himself, "he kept the chicken yard at the Hermitage in an uproar."

When Jackson was a senator in Washington in 1824, his letters to Rachel showed some concern for the boy's behavior. "Tell Lyncoya I expect him to be a good boy and to hear from you when I come home that he has been so in my absence, and has learned his Book well," Jackson wrote.

But Jackson trusted the boy implicitly, and sent him on errands with important papers and large amounts of money. Jackson had plans for taking the boy to Washington, introducing him to the secretary of war, and getting him into the military academy, but he had to give up those plans when a new administration came into power.

Jackson decided that Lincoya should learn a trade, so the two of them—the world-famous hero of the Battle of New Orleans and the fourteen-year-old Indian boy—made a special trip to Nashville to visit a variety of shops and see what appealed most to Lincoya. The boy chose to work in a saddler's shop, and was apprenticed to a Nashville saddlemaker in 1827. He spent every weekend at the Hermitage, and Jackson gave him one of his fine horses to ride to and from Nashville.

Confinement in the shop did not agree with Lincoya, and in a few months he took a cold that "settled in his lungs." He went home to the Hermitage, where Rachel gave him the best of care, but Lincoya died on June 1, 1828, when he was only sixteen. It was the first death at the Hermitage, and there is no record of where he was buried. Some say it was in the same garden where Rachel Jackson was buried a few months later.

Jackson was in the midst of his campaign for the presidency when Lincoya died. He had with him at the Hermitage, helping write some of his campaign speeches, one of the most tragic and gifted figures of American history, Henry "Black Horse Harry" Lee, older half-brother of Robert E. Lee.

Henry Lee, who knew Lincoya well, was so moved at his death that he laid aside campaign speeches to write a tribute, now lost, that has been called a "precious pearl of poetry in prose." For Lee saw the grief of the tall general who had fed an orphaned baby on a bloody battlefield.

Pretty Peggy Eaton

Blue-eyed Peggy Eaton, with her dazzling smile and exquisite figure, admitted she liked to worry people—innocently, of course. Little things like wearing one red shoe and one black shoe at the same time. It amused her to see stiff-necked wives of senators from the hinterland gape at her.

But split the cabinet! Or bring the government to a standstill! Never would she dream of such a thing, she pouted sweetly. Yet that was precisely her role in history.

Never in the history of the United States has one woman so shaken the country with scandal. "Peggy O'Neale" (her maiden name) and "Peggy Eaton" became synonyms for shocking behavior. "Nice" ladies turned on their heels when she came near.

Peggy's Tennessee husband, John Henry Eaton of Franklin, resigned his cabinet job as secretary of war because of the scandal. President Andrew Jackson, barely in the White House when the furor broke, saw the first year and a half of his administration almost wrecked by it. He had beaten the British, defeated Indians, and out-maneuvered politicians, but he could do little about spitfire Peggy—bewitching in her lacy flounces and satin shoes. When the battle over Peggy shifted to Tennessee and split Jackson's own family, the old warrior was shattered, in tears.

Peggy, born in Washington, daughter of an innkeeper who was host to top men in government, had grown up on politics.

Senators had jogged her on their knees when she was an infant. Ambassadors, congressmen, and cabinet members had turned her head with compliments when she was still a schoolgirl.

She had turned down various distinguished suitors before at eighteen she married a handsome young navy officer named John Timberlake. They had three children (one died in infancy), and Timberlake himself died when Peggy was thirty-one. Four months later she married Tennessee Sen. John Eaton, "the handsomest man in Washington," she said. Already tongues were wagging.

Eaton had stayed at Peggy's father's inn (actually a seventy-room hotel called the Franklin House, halfway between the capitol and Georgetown) from the time he became a senator, in 1818. He was twenty-eight years old then, a widower himself (his first wife, Myra Lewis, was a ward of Andrew Jackson). He became a close friend of Peggy's entire family—her husband, her father, her mother. Gossip had it that Eaton and Peggy were on more than friendly terms before her husband died.

Eaton had been in the Senate six years when Jackson came there as senator in 1823 and also moved into the Franklin House. The two of them were often invited to share Sunday evening with the family of the innkeeper, William O'Neale, in their handsome home across the street. Jackson wrote home to Rachel about those Sunday evenings when pretty Peggy entertained: "Mrs. Timberlake . . . plays on the Piano Delightfully, and every Sunday evening entertains her pious mother with Sacred music to which we are invited."

Timberlake gave up his navy career just after his marriage, but his business failed and he returned to sea. He helped his father-in-law meet a pressing debt, and Eaton—close friend of both men—advanced a loan that tided them over the financial crisis. Years later, gossips seized on that fact to make it appear that Eaton was getting repaid through Peggy's favors.

While Timberlake was at sea, he kept up a friendly correspondence with the Tennessee senator. Only six days before he died, on a Mediterranean island, the ailing Timberlake wrote Peggy: "In case anything should happen to me, there is only one man to whose hands I should be willing to entrust you, and that is John H. Eaton."

It was Eaton who, by chance, was given the message of Timberlake's death, and he had to break the news to Peggy.

Three months later, in November, 1828, he proposed to her. People were already whispering about his attentiveness to the "tavern-keeper's daughter." When Eaton asked Jackson if he thought it too soon to marry the pretty widow, the president-elect told him to "marry her and shut their mouths" if he loved her.

Margaret O'Neale Timberlake and John H. Eaton were married on January 1, 1829, only a few days after Rachel Jackson's death at the Hermitage. By the time Jackson got to Washington, the scene was set for embarrassment by his appointment of Eaton to the cabinet.

Peggy, in a not altogether reliable autobiography she wrote as an old woman, insisted that the first hint of the gossip about her came at a ball the British ambassador gave only two months after her marriage. The gossips were saying that she was expecting Eaton's child when she married him. Furthermore, gossip had it, Eaton would turn down the job of minister to France because his pregnant wife could not stand the voyage. Peggy was furious. She told Eaton to turn down the job so they could stay in Washington and show their detractors that she was not pregnant. As a matter of fact, Peggy and Eaton never had any children.

President Jackson was beside himself when he heard the tales. Instead of making Eaton minister to France, he made him secretary of war. Jackson's own wife, Rachel, had died only two months before, after years of torment from politicians who tried to smear her name. And now his good friend Eaton had to see his wife's reputation damaged by politicians. Jackson set his jaw in grim determination. He would battle it out with Vice-President John C. Calhoun and those cabinet members who had set about to freeze Eaton out of the cabinet.

Eaton, who had written a biography of Jackson that was used in the Tennessean's campaign for the presidency, had been almost like a son to Jackson. There were politicians, both in Tennessee and in Washington, who were jealous of Eaton's influence with Jackson. If they could cause a rift between the two men, it could wreck Jackson's cabinet.

Jackson told Peggy not to worry about the gossips. It was only their way of getting at him. But she was furious when her husband told her that Jackson had set detectives to work to track down every story about her. She stormed into the White House the next morning to confront the president: "Am I become a chambermaid that recommendations of my character should be sought where I have been? . . . I want you to know, sir, that . . . I do not want endorsements any more than any other lady in the land."

Jackson tried to quiet her. He was doing it, he said, to prove to all her detractors that they were liars. But high-tempered Peggy flew out of the White House in a huff. She fumed and wept. She felt that even her good friend the president no longer had confidence in her. "I never was so hurt in my life," she wrote years later. "It seemed to me an outrage committed by my dearest and best friend."

Eaton, a gentle soul with remarkable patience, tried to

reason with her. The president, he told her, was trying to protect her from more vicious slander than she had imagined. Impetuous Peggy drove back to the White House to apologize to Jackson for her outburst, and later Jackson called at the War Department to congratulate Eaton on his wife's spunk.

So began a year and a half of tearful and stormy scenes in the White House—scenes when Jackson lectured his niece and nephew about how to treat Peggy; scenes when the cabinet sat icily silent while Jackson told them how to treat Peggy; scenes when the grieving Jackson wept through the night because nobody would listen to him.

The slaps at Peggy mounted into a great crescendo of spite, official and personal. No "nice" lady in Washington would call on the Eatons. Cabinet wives announced that they would not attend even White House dinners if "that woman" were there. Newspapers brought the scandal into the open, declaring that it was a "pity that Jackson had appointed Eaton to his cabinet when rumors about Mrs. Eaton make it clear she is not fitted to the role of cabinet wife."

"I boiled," Peggy said. "I felt outraged. I wanted to shoot Duff Green (the editor) outright."

Washington was in a broiling debate about Peggy's virtue. Was she guilty or not? No historian will go out on a limb on the matter. Even in Nashville and Franklin, where Peggy and her husband were widely entertained, their hosts' descendants disagree on the issue. Some defend her; others lift their eyebrows at mention of her name.

But Peggy, tenacious as a bulldog, denied all and vowed to track down the story herself.

Starting at the top to get to the bottom of the scandal about her, Peggy stormed into the White House and demanded that President Jackson tell her who was spreading the gossip. Was it a Philadelphia preacher, as she had heard?

Was he the one who had said she was unfaithful to her first husband and was carrying her second husband's child before they were married?

Yes, Jackson said, it was the preacher. Peggy demanded to know exactly what the preacher had said. Jackson asked if she remembered a carriage ride with Eaton when she was still married to her first husband, John Timberlake. Peggy did. She and her mother had accepted Eaton's invitation to go for a drive to try out a new carriage. When the horses bolted and ran away, all passengers were thrown out and the carriage wrecked. Another carriage took the bruised passengers home.

What was wrong with that? Peggy's mother, a dignified and pious woman, had been with them every moment.

Jackson told Peggy to go home and worry no more. He had been a friend of Eaton's for twenty years and knew him to be an honorable man. He was also aware of how carefully Peggy had been brought up. Jackson had, in fact, encouraged Eaton to marry her. Wasn't that evidence enough of his confidence in her?

But that did not satisfy her. A few days later, when Eaton and Jackson were away from Washington, Peggy accompanied her parents to Philadelphia, where she sought out the gossipy preacher, Rev. Ezra Ely (President John Q. Adams called him a "busybody Presbyterian preacher").

For six hours she raged at him, demanding that he tell her what stories he had distributed. He finally revealed the source of his information: another Presbyterian preacher, Rev. John N. Campbell, pastor of a Washington church.

"Good God!" Peggy shouted. "Can it be possible that . . . the clergy have taken upon themselves to tear reputations to pieces rather than to perform the part of the peace maker?"

Reverend Ely told Peggy that Reverend Campbell had heard the gossip from Dr. Elijah Craven, a Washington physician who had been dead for years. The physician and his family had been friends of Peggy's family, but he had never been their doctor.

The story, as relayed through the two ministers, was this: At the time of the runaway carriage accident, Dr. Craven had been called to Peggy's home to treat her; there a cackling old woman who he *supposed* was Peggy's mother had laughed boisterously and told him he arrived too late to take care of Peggy's miscarriage. The scandal was that Peggy's husband, a navy officer, had been out of the country for more than a year. The accusation: the child would have been Eaton's.

Peggy flew into a blind fury. She had never had a miscarriage in her life, she screamed. She had never been guilty of any wrongdoing with John Eaton. She had been faithful to John Timberlake as long as he lived. Furthermore, she said, the whole story was outrageously out of keeping with the character of her mother. Dr. Craven had known her mother well. He would have had no doubt who she was.

Before Peggy left Reverend Ely, he promised to write President Jackson to tell him he was convinced the story was untrue. But he never did.

When Peggy returned to Washington, she and Eaton confronted Reverend Campbell. Peggy demanded to know when the miscarriage was supposed to have occurred. The minister said promptly and definitely that it was in 1821.

Peggy sent a messenger to the Navy Department, nearby, to get certain records. The records showed that in 1821 Timberlake was in Washington, at the time of the supposed miscarriage and for more than a year before.

"There is a mistake in the navy record," the minister said, "or else it was another year." Peggy, enraged, lashed out at the minister, "reeled and fell," and struck her head against a sofa, but she pulled her husband back just before he struck the cowering minister.

That night President Jackson came calling on the Eatons. He wanted to know if Peggy had the record books her first husband had kept during the four years he ran a store in Washington—years he was *not* in the navy. Peggy got them, and Jackson sat down in the Eaton parlor to study them. Sure enough, the date of the supposed miscarriage came during the time Timberlake was operating the store.

When Dr. Craven's wife and mother told Peggy they never heard him mention any such incident, Peggy was convinced the Presbyterian ministers had made up the story at the urging of political enemies. Jackson had evidence that Vice-President John C. Calhoun and Henry Clay, with a "traitorous clique of three Judases" in the cabinet, were chief purveyors of the story. They were whipping the breeze into a whirlwind.

The social snubs continued. The Dutch minister's wife announced that she would give a formal dinner and cut the Eatons dead by inviting every cabinet member and his wife except them. The wives of the "three Judases" planned to follow up with a series of state dinners to which all top officials except the Eatons would be asked.

Jackson—red-eyed after a sleepless night—instructed Martin Van Buren, his secretary of state, to tell the Dutch minister to call off the dinner or return to Holland. The battle over Peggy had become an international issue. What control did the president have over an ambassador's guest list? Jackson laid down the law: when the host failed to treat cabinet members equally, he was meddling in our internal affairs.

Peggy got in her licks. At a ball where she dazzled guests

with her beauty and grace, she saw them scatter when she danced near. She made it a game, aiming straight at every congested area of the dance floor and clearing it like a firecracker.

Jackson called cabinet meetings specifically to deal with the Peggy Eaton matter. Either they would act as a unit, attending to the nation's business, or he would get a new cabinet. He made a point of giving a state dinner at the White House in honor of Peggy. At cabinet dinners, he regularly placed her at his right and out-glared the women who glared at her.

Jackson had no rest from the ugly business in his own household. With no relatives of his own, he had lavished affection on his wife's nieces and nephews. He had taken one of the latter, Andrew Jackson Donelson, to the White House as his private secretary, and had made Donelson's wife, Emily, his official hostess. It was a bitter blow when they sided against Jackson.

The Donelsons' tiffs with Jackson over Peggy were numerous and bitter. By the time they were packing to leave Washington for a summer in Nashville in 1830, Jackson laid down the law: he would leave them in Tennessee if they continued to behave as they had. There would be no more White House for them.

But when they got to Nashville, Jackson was horrified to see that the Peggy Eaton affair was the hottest political issue. Families were split on the matter, old political allies were cool to him, and icy silences settled over friends gathered around hospitable dinners at the Hermitage.

At one of them, when top political figures of the state were barely civil to Eaton and his wife, Peggy saw Jackson slip away from the men having brandy and cigars in the parlor. Eaton sent his wife to look for the president, and she found him lying across his wife's grave. He was weeping, he told Peggy, at the memory of insults Rachel had suffered from politicians.

Peggy, meantime, was storing up choice stories of Tennessee society to titillate Washington parties. A great mimic, she told later about a formal dinner Judge John Overton, Jackson's closest friend, gave for them at his home, Travellers' Rest.

"After dinner," she said, "the custom was for the ladies to retire while the gentlemen drank their wine and smoked their cigars. We followed Mrs. Overton upstairs—I remember the white oak stairs. The ladies entered a circular room when I saw what was to me an inexplicable sight. Chairs were put all around a table for as many ladies as there were in the party. Small boxes were on the table, and to each box a twig . . . about four inches long . . . and beside each chair there sat a wash basin. I suppose my amazement at this sight must have shown itself on my face, for the other ladies were obviously amused at my embarrassed ignorance. At last I said, 'What does this mean?'"

Mrs. Edward Breathitt, sister of Eaton and wife of Franklin's mayor, said. "Look here, Sister, if you expect Brother to keep his politica position in Tennessee, you have got to dip."

Peggy professed never to have heard the term. "Dip?" she said. "Mary Breathitt, *dip*? What do you mean by that?"

The ladies "roared," Peggy said, when they saw she thought she was to "dip" in the wash basin. Then Mrs. Overton, "a woman of bland speech though of much manners," instructed Peggy on chewing a twig, dipping it in the snuff, then "rubbing away at your teeth with all your might."

Peggy said she was game. She could do anything the Tennessee ladies could do.

She "rubbed away" until, all of a sudden, the reaction hit.

"The house seemed to me to be a little unsteady," Peggy said. "The walls did not sit stiff. Things began to go round." She became violently nauseated, and ruined her fine silk dress with its Honiton lace.

"You should have heard those women scream," Peggy said. "They were filled with laughter. They leaned against the wall and upon the table and roared. Mrs. Judge Overton simply laid down upon the floor and roared."

Peggy's exaggeration was part of her storytelling charm, and her own laughter was uninhibited. Her vocabulary, she admitted, was blunt and full of Anglo-Saxon vigor. She had no patience with "soft Latin phrases."

The Eatons made their headquarters at Franklin that summer—part of the time at his mother's home and part of the time at Eaton's own home, where Franklin's Catholic church stands today. Next door was the Masonic Hall (still standing), where the Episcopal church was holding its services then, and Peggy played the organ there on Sunday mornings.

Jackson was delighted at the way Franklin people received Peggy. No matter what they thought of her, they had the good manners to treat her well. When he rode out to Franklin on horseback, unannounced, one July afternoon, he found that "between 300 and 500 of Major Eaton's old neighbors and friends" were honoring Eaton with a barbecue. Jackson observed that the courtesy of Franklin citizens was "severe comment on the combination at Nashville."

All through the summer of 1830, when Tennessee was torn by anger and spite over the Peggy affair, Jackson conferred frequently with political leaders at Eaton's home, at Travellers' Rest, and at the Hermitage. Jackson tried to persuade Eaton to leave Peggy in Franklin with his mother for at least part of the winter. With the "petticoat government" out of sight, perhaps Washington could get on with its business.

Besides, Jackson had heard the latest slander from Washington: Peggy was "running the White House"; she was the "Madame Pompadour" (politically powerful mistress of Louis XV of France) of Jackson's administration.

Jackson bridled at the inference. "Mrs. Eaton, like all others, may have her imprudencies," he said of the hot-tempered beauty with the thick brown hair. "Let them be considered as improprieties, but not treated as a lady without virtue."

Peggy did go back to Washington, though, and the "get Eaton" campaign got hotter. Jackson's health almost cracked under the strain of a year of wrangling with the cabinet, and with Donelson about letting Emily return.

Some historians say Peggy helped place Martin Van Buren in the White House. At any rate, as secretary of state, he steered a course in the Peggy Eaton affair that proved his loyalty to Jackson and won Jackson's backing as the man to succeed him.

Jackson was so depressed over the hopeless muddle in his cabinet and his household that Van Buren was afraid to bring bad news. But in the spring of 1831, during a horseback ride, he found the moment to suggest a solution: he would resign and pave the way for a new cabinet. Reluctantly, Jackson agreed to it. Then Eaton decided to make his resignation official the day before Van Buren's, and Jackson was at last rid of the burden of Peggy.

The president said he was envious of the Eatons when they returned to Tennessee in November, 1831. The governor and legislature welcomed them in a "flattering reception," and there were triumphant dinners at Franklin and Murfreesboro.

Eaton, settled in his comfortable Franklin home to practice law and operate his farm, at first enjoyed retirement
from public life. But he soon ran for senator, was defeated,
and by 1834 was appointed governor of the territory of
Florida. Two years later, when Eaton was made minister to
Spain, Peggy entered Madrid's court circle for the four most
glorious years of her life. She swished in and out of the royal
palace as friend and confidante of the queen, and knew she
could never be satisfied with life in Tennessee again.

After Eaton's service in Spain ended, he practiced law
in Washington and lived comfortably there until his death
in 1856. For twenty-six years Peggy had been a devoted
wife to Eaton. Now, at fifty-seven, she was surrounded by
the orphaned grandchildren she was raising.

Her vanity was her undoing. At age sixty-one she married
her grandchildren's dancing master, Antonio Buchignani, an
Italian immigrant who was nineteen years old at the time.
For seven years she supported the handsome youth, decking
him out like a paper doll and parading him about Washington
in a pathetic show. Then he tricked her out of her home and
her estate of ninety thousand dollars, and eloped to Europe
with Peggy's sixteen-year-old granddaughter.

Poverty-stricken, dependent on a young grandson who
earned meager pay as a government clerk, Peggy held her
head high as she flounced out of her shabby apartment and
down Pennsylvania Avenue for brisk walks among her
glamorous ghosts almost to the day she died, at age eighty,
in November, 1879.

Even at the Hermitage, where the Eatons were often
guests and where they stood vigil while Jackson died, Peggy's
portrait today does not rate a place in the "big house." Instead, it hangs in the board room, in a wing of the custodian's
home, out of the public's sight.

"Black Horse Harry" Lee

How the Hermitage, Andrew Jackson's home, became refuge for Robert E. Lee's brother when scandal and poverty hounded him out of his Virginia home is a story long lost among the skeletons in history's closets. But it brought Nashville close to the heart of the Confederate hero and his unfortunate half-brother.

Actually, the overwhelming tragedy of Henry Lee's life occurred when his baby brother, Robert, was so young that he would scarcely have realized what was wrong. Henry Lee was a college student, twenty years old, when Robert E. Lee was born on January 19, 1807.

Their father was George Washington's friend and favorite officer in the Revolutionary War, the dashing cavalry leader "Light Horse Harry" Lee. Henry Lee, born at the family's ancient Virginia home, Stratford, had spent his childhood there and in the governor's mansion in Richmond, when his father was governor.

Educated at Washington College in Lexington, Virginia, and at William and Mary College in Williamsburg, Henry entered politics immediately and was elected to the Virginia state legislature for three successive terms. When the War of 1812 began, he was commissioned a major in the army and served under Gen. Andrew Jackson, whom he was not to meet until many years later.

When the war was over, Major Lee stayed for a while in

New York, where he was much in demand in the city's social circles. Witty and debonair, he was "much sought after in society," one writer of the day recorded.

No portrait of him exists, probably because "Black Horse Harry" so blackened his own name that no one cared to perpetuate the memory. But there are many descriptions of him as "not handsome, but one of the most attractive men in conversation we ever listened to."

He was a "brilliant conversationalist, the charm of old and young alike save when a satirical spirit seasoned his talk too heavily with sarcasm," another friend wrote.

How much his father's tragic last years had to do with Henry Lee's cynicism can only be surmised. In any case, at the very time when Henry Lee was in college and most sensitive to criticism, his distinguished father suffered the humiliation of being thrown into debtors' prison for two years. The dispirited Revolutionary War hero and former governor died a pauper far from home, the victim of political enemies and his own generous spirit. The only reason that he had not lost the three-thousand-acre estate at Stratford was that the property had come to him through his first wife, and she had willed it to their son, Henry.

The old general's second wife and her five children, including Robert E. Lee, had left the mansion and moved to a small home in Alexandria, Virginia, several years before the general died in 1818. Henry Lee had taken possession of Stratford two years before his father died and the property became legally his. The house was terribly run down, and it was only when Henry married, in 1817, that he, with his young bride—the wealthiest girl in Virginia—redecorated the historic mansion and furnished it luxuriously.

The bride, Anne McCarty, was a neighbor of the Lees, having grown up on the adjoining plantation. She and her younger sister, Elizabeth, had inherited a vast tobacco and thoroughbred plantation, and interest in a brick-making industry. Orphaned as small children and brought up by their grandmother, the girls were sent to finishing school in Philadelphia and presented to society in Washington. It was there that Henry Lee, himself a favorite in Washington society, first took note of the regal Miss McCarty.

"Your neighbor, Miss McCarty, has been here dashing in a fine carriage," one of Henry Lee's friends wrote him from Washington in March, 1816. The following March, Miss McCarty and Henry Lee were married. He was thirty years old and his bride nineteen. She was handsome with black hair, dark eyes, arched brows, and her high spirits set a new pace at Stratford.

Suddenly the forbidding old walls were transformed. There were house parties, hunting parties, and balls, and the elegance of Stratford entertaining outshone anything in the countryside. Life there was so merry that Anne's younger sister, sixteen-year-old Elizabeth, decided to move in and enjoy the gay seasons. Her stepfather had been her guardian for years, controlling her vast properties, but she took legal steps to have Henry Lee appointed her guardian instead.

In the fall of 1818 the only child of Anne and Henry Lee was born. The baby's tragic death two years later led to ruin of the whole family, and the end of Stratford for the Lees. In early 1820, two-year-old Margaret Lee was killed when she tumbled down the steep flight of stone steps leading from the front entrance of the mansion. (Strangely enough, it was on the same flight of steps four generations earlier that another heir to Stratford, little Philip Ludwell Lee, had fallen to his death.)

Anne McCarty Lee was inconsolable. In grief over her daughter's death she began to depend on morphine to deaden the hours. Soon she was a "hopeless" addict, shut in her room and quite beyond the reach of her household.

The gloom that enveloped Stratford struck so suddenly that Elizabeth McCarty was stunned. A short, plump, even-tempered girl who loved music, poetry, and flowers—as well as parties—Elizabeth had only her brother-in-law's company as they roamed the sad house.

Day after day, month after month, Henry Lee and Elizabeth were thrown "into a state of the most unguarded intimacy," as Henry himself explained later. The scandal that was being whispered over the countryside came into the open when Elizabeth bore Henry a child.

In Westmoreland County, seat of Stratford, tradition has it that the illegitimate child of Henry Lee and Elizabeth died at birth. At any rate, the scandal shook Virginia society to its foundations. Henry's political and social careers were ended. Elizabeth withdrew into hermitlike seclusion, shrouding herself in penitence the rest of her long life.

Her first move was to return to her own home and take steps to have her stepfather made her legal guardian again. That involved nine years of litigation and wrecked Henry Lee's already sad finances, for he had dipped into Elizabeth's holdings to bolster up his own.

Part of Elizabeth's penitence was to cut her gorgeous brown hair. The rest of her life she wore it cropped short. And for the rest of her life she wore mourning, and never left her home except to go to church or to care for the sick.

Meantime, Henry Lee, staggering under the blow of public disgrace and poverty, was forced to sell Stratford, the home of his ancestors for six generations. His wife stayed at Stratford only long enough to sign her name to the deed passing the estate out of the Lee family forever.

She left her husband and went to Tennessee, to a health resort near Nashville, to try to break the "dope" habit. Called the Fountain of Health, the resort, near the Hermitage, was known throughout the South for its beneficent springs. While taking the cure there, Anne Lee met Rachel and Andrew Jackson and was often a guest in their home. And Henry Lee kept writing Anne of his deep penitence.

He moved to Fredericksburg, about forty miles from Stratford, and settled down to writing a history. But in Fredericksburg, as in Washington and Richmond, the doors of former friends were closed to him. In desperate need of money, he tried to get government jobs, but all jobs were closed to him. One of the first to support Andrew Jackson for the presidency, Lee was horrified to learn that his very enthusiasm for the Tennessean had been used by Jackson's enemies for propaganda purposes against him.

Lee was so shocked at that turn of events that he wrote a long letter to Jackson in 1825, explaining what had occurred since he became "an active friend of your election." Immediately Jackson wrote Lee, inviting him to visit him at the Hermitage. There began one of the strongest friendships of Lee's life.

Jackson put Lee to work at writing his official letters and speeches and his campaign messages. Lee undertook writing a biography of Jackson, and was one of his closest advisers throughout Jackson's campaign for the presidency in 1828.

Meanwhile, Anne Lee had broken herself of the drug habit, and it is said that Andrew and Rachel Jackson had a part in effecting a reconciliation between Anne and Henry Lee. For a while both of them lived at the Fountain of Health. Then they moved to a little house "within 2 & 1/2 miles of Nashville," Lee said, where the still-ailing Anne could be near a doctor.

The Lees were much with Jackson during Rachel's last illness, and Henry Lee had to hurry from her funeral to help Jackson polish up his inauguration speech. Lee accompanied the sorrowing Jackson to Washington for his inauguration and remained with him for a time.

Jackson's attempts to get Lee back on his feet again were touching. Over and over he appointed him to public office, but everywhere the old scandal rose to haunt Henry Lee. Vengeful politicians saw to it that no appointments were approved.

At length Jackson offered Lee the most unwanted, dangerous job in the consular service: consul to Algiers. The life of a white man was constantly in jeopardy there, but Lee gladly accepted the post, and Anne gladly faced the dangers with him.

After a spectacularly successful year in which Lee was hero in several encounters with the natives, the U.S. Senate became aware of his appointment for the first time. Reviving the old scandal, they voted not to approve the appointment, and he was recalled.

That was the shattering blow for Henry and Anne. They knew at last that there was nothing for them in America. Lee was forty-three and Anne thirty-two when they packed their trunks to leave Algiers in August, 1830, and try to build a new life in Italy or France.

Lee had brought along his father's official papers of the Revolutionary War period, and in Paris he settled down to complete the history his father had begun in debtors' prison. When the volume was published, it was so filled with bitterness toward Thomas Jefferson and others who had made life miserable for his father that the main effect of the book was to make new enemies for the author.

But when Lee wrote the first of his two-volume biography

of Napoleon, it was an instant success. He had almost finished the second volume when he fell victim to an influenza epidemic that struck Paris in 1837.

Henry Lee, forty-nine years old, died January 30, 1837, and was buried in an unmarked grave at Montmartre in Paris. Anne, stranded in Paris without money or friends, could not bring herself to write even her husband's brother, Carter Lee, about the death for weeks.

Two months later she wrote a Nashville friend about it. "The death of my dear husband was so sudden, so unexpected . . . ," she wrote Maj. William B. Lewis. "The blow fell on me with overwhelming force. . . . There never was a better heart beat in a human bosom than his, nor a more noble and generous spirit bowed down by neglect and mortification."

Moving to even cheaper quarters in Paris, Anne Lee tried to pay off her husband's debts, and had only his pathetic little dog, Cora, for company. Crippled with rheumatism, in bed most of the time, Anne wrote one last pitiful letter to Carter Lee, stating that her rent was paid but she had only a few francs left. "When that is gone, what is to become of me?" the woman who had once been the richest girl in Virginia wrote. "I have no friend on earth but you."

Three years after her husband's death, Anne Lee died and was buried in an unmarked grave in Paris. Only her "petit chien" was with her at the time of her death.

Far away in Virginia, her sister Elizabeth lived out her lonely years—in Stratford, ironically enough. She had married a neighboring farmer, and he had bought the decaying Stratford at public auction.

But there was no gaiety the second time Elizabeth moved to Stratford. In mourning and seclusion even after her marriage, Elizabeth grew herbs for medicinal purposes, and her remedies were the standby of the community. She would have been happy to send money to Anne, her relatives said, but Anne refused to communicate with her after the illegitimate baby's birth.

Elizabeth had no other children. Left a widow eighteen years after her marriage, she lived on at Stratford for thirty-five years more, until her death in 1879. Ironically, she had owned the place longer than anyone else in its history. For over half a century she busied herself in house and garden as mistress of the great, gaunt Stratford, whose downfall had come with her own.

She played the piano and sang, and read a great deal in the empty house. She grew quite religious, and talked of her rose and herb garden when visitors came. She always wore white inside the house, black outside. And at seventy-nine she completed her fifty-eight years of atonement.

Matthew Fontaine Maury
and the Seas

The Sunday morning that Matthew Fontaine Maury threw his leg across a borrowed horse to ride from his father's Williamson County farm and join the navy, the gloom hung heavy. That was in 1825, and no one—with the possible exception of the schoolmaster who had lent Maury the money to make the trip—could have imagined that the curly-haired youth would someday catch the oceans by their bottoms and shake out mysteries that no sea captain had ever fathomed.

Like a giant with legs twelve miles long, Maury strode the seas to scoop up answers to ocean riddles that still awe scientists. A dreamer, a poet with as practical a mind as ever worked out a mathematical formula, he discovered "machinery" in the ocean depths that no admiral in the navy had ever seen.

He dropped weighted lines to the bottom of the seas and mapped drowned mountains and valleys where submarine navigators wind their shadowy way today and plot the course of future wars under the sea. He traced the paths of whales between arctic oceans a hundred years ago, and discovered the route that the atomic submarine *Seadragon* snaked under the icebergs from Baffin Bay to the Bering Sea in August, 1960.

He trailed weights to the ocean floor to discover the underwater plateau that connects Newfoundland with Ireland, and so made it possible to lay the first cable tying

America to Europe. That cable was forerunner of all telephone and radio communication between the two continents.

He dipped a thermometer deep into the seas to trace the
borders of a warm river, the Gulf Stream, that rushes uphill
through icy oceans, and he outlined broad "highways" where
ships could span oceans in a fraction of the time previously
required. He clocked the winds to chart air currents that
guide pilots on round-the-world flights today. He measured
the motion of clouds above and waters below to discover the
"perfectly balanced mechanism" for air-conditioning the
globe.

"The atmosphere . . . is an engine which pumps our rivers
up from the sea, and carries them through the clouds to their
sources in the mountains," Maury wrote. "Air and water are
the great agents of the sun in distributing heat over the surface of the globe, cooling this climate and tempering that;
and in this light, I propose to consider the winds and allude
to the currents of the sea."

The United States Weather Bureau grew, in large part, out
of his work. The U.S. Naval Observatory in Washington grew
out of his work. Our West was settled more rapidly because
of the months he cut off sailing time between New York and
San Francisco by his guides to smooth sea-highways.

He brought shippers of eighteen nations together in
a "summit conference" in Brussels to initiate one of the
tremendous research projects of all history, a study involving
thousands of ships on all seas. His work brought millions in
gold to shippers around the world when his clearly marked
"paths" cut in two the time it took to get merchandise from
one continent to another.

Kings decorated him, merchants feted him. An island
was named for him. Statues in many countries commemorate
his mammoth conquest of the seas. His books and lectures on

the subject so captivated the suddenly science-minded world that he was mentioned in 1859 as candidate for president of the United States.

But no medals hung on Maury's coat the spring morning in 1825 when he rode a white horse from his father's farm, near Franklin, Tennessee, to begin the five-hundred-mile journey to Washington. Not even a father's good-bye blessed the departure, for Richard Maury turned his back as his nineteen-year-old son, Matthew, rode away.

Only one year earlier, Matthew's older brother, Midshipman John Minor Maury, had died of yellow fever on shipboard and was buried in the Atlantic. With that sorrow still heavy on the family's heart, Matthew made all arrangements for going to sea without consulting his father. Sam Houston, then congressman from Tennessee, was a friend of the family, and young Matthew had appealed to him for the appointment as midshipman.

"The first intelligence my parents had of my intentions was this letter of appointment," Maury wrote later. "It had disturbed the family very much, and my father expressed his disapprobation of my conduct in strong terms. As I had proceeded without consulting him, he determined to leave me to my own resources. I was resolute. I got a man to trust me with a horse until I could remit him the money after selling it in Virginia. I set out from home without a cent in my pocket, intending to trust to luck, and, if necessary, stop on the road and work out my bills when I got to town."

The slight, brown-haired youth had yearned to find out more about the world ever since he brought shoes home from a Franklin shoemaker's shop and noticed strange markings scratched on the rough soles.

"Old Mr. Neil," the village cobbler, had explained to puzzled Matthew that it was part of a science known as algebra—the key to all sorts of scientific problems. "He worked out his problems with his awl on leather, and would send home shoes with their soles covered with little x's and y's," Matthew recalled years later. "My earliest recollections of ambition in science are connected with the aspiration to emulate that man in mathematics."

Born on January 14, 1806, on his father's farm near Fredericksburg, Virginia, Matthew Fontaine Maury was five years old when he moved with his parents to Williamson County. His father's cousin, Abram Maury, had moved there fourteen years earlier and founded the town of Franklin. (He turned down the idea of having the town named in his honor, but allowed the neighboring county to carry his name.)

When Matthew Maury attended the one-room school miles down the road from the farm, he preferred books to hoes and plows. When he was twelve years old and injured his back in a fall from a tree, Matthew saw an advantage: his father decided that he would no longer be fitted for farm work. Instead, he would attend the scholarly Harpeth Academy, near Franklin, so that he could earn a living by brain power.

It was the first in a series of "misfortunes" that paved the way for young Maury's success. At Harpeth Academy, his teachers were powerful men who shook his mind with the wonders of the world: James Otey, later to become first Episcopal bishop in Tennessee; Dr. Gideon Blackburn, famed educator and churchman; William G. Hasbrouck, eventually a distinguished lawyer in New York.

Starry-eyed Matthew Maury, through all the honors that foreign empires heaped on in later years, looked back gratefully on those "Tennessee school days when the air was filled with castles." It was Hasbrouck, the teacher, who advanced

Maury thirty dollars at the last minute to help finance the trip to Washington.

Maury had planned from the first to stop in Fredericks-burg, Virginia, his birthplace, to visit uncles and cousins. Robert E. Lee, his friend in later life, had been born a few miles from Fredericksburg only a year after Maury's birth, and the village was rich with the elegance of Washingtons and Lees, the aristocracy of Virginia.

Young Maury, straight from the Tennessee frontier, had never seen ice cream until his Virginia cousins served it, and he, thinking it a sauce, dipped a little from his dish and passed the rest around the table. But the rosy-cheeked farm boy caught the eye of one of his Virginia cousins, Ann Herndon, a young beauty whom he married nine years later. Already, on that first trip from his father's farm, Matthew's future was being settled.

Luck held when he reached Washington. At navy head-quarters he found the travel allowance much higher than he had imagined. He drew enough money to repay his old teacher and finish paying for the horse, and had enough left over to live on until he drew his first navy pay.

His first ship was something special. General Lafayette had just finished a sentimental tour of the United States, and a new ship had been named in honor of the famed battle the French hero had helped our Revolutionary War soldiers win. The old general was to return to France on the U.S. frigate *Brandywine*, and an escort of midshipmen from every state would accompany him. Young Maury represented Tennessee on the glamorous mission.

It was September 8, 1825, when Lafayette boarded the ship near Washington, and the crowd gathered there for the farewell ceremony thought it a spectacular omen when the ship sailed off through a brilliant rainbow to Chesapeake Bay and the Atlantic. But the voyage was a rough one—so rough, in fact, that the midshipmen hardly caught sight of the seasick Lafayette. Maury began to worry about how much he was going to learn from instructors stationed on the ship to train fledgling naval officers (a system used before the Navy Academy was established).

When Lafayette debarked at Le Havre and the crew settled down for a training cruise about the Mediterranean, Maury realized how inadequate the ship's library was. At every port, he snooped around bookstalls for guides on navigation. In Spain he found an excellent book on navigation, bought a Spanish dictionary, and learned language and navigation at the same time. In his bunk, he would memorize sentences that meant nothing to him, and work them out while he stood watch.

"I used to draw problems in spherical trigonometry with chalk and put them in the racks where I could see them as I walked the deck," he recalled years later.

Before the nine-month cruise was over, word got around that Maury could work any navigation problem. Other midshipmen amused themselves by speculating on whether Maury would someday become admiral.

After a brief visit to his Tennessee home, he sailed for South America. Endless curiosity about every land he visited—animal life, vegetation, weather, land formations, fossils, customs, and languages—led him to exotic adventures on rocky crags and in steamy jungles.

Three years later, on a round-the-world cruise, he discovered a savage Pacific-island tribe that his dead brother had once befriended. Matthew Maury also was able to save the chieftain from enemies, and in return he offered Maury "his scepter, his own wife, and the daughter of a neighboring chieftain if I would remain," Maury wrote.

On another voyage, just before Maury sailed from a South American port, a young Chilean officer called on him to inform him that a belle of Valparaiso had refused to marry him because she hoped to marry Maury. A few months later Maury was distressed to learn that the girl had died.

But he had never forgotten the Virginia girl he met four years before in Fredericksburg. When he reached home June 28, 1830—a polished young officer with four years of cruising and study under the navy's top officers—he was determined to look up the lovely Ann Herndon. They were engaged before he went to sea again, in June, 1831, this time on the most fateful voyage of his life.

For Maury was sailing master on the *Falmouth*, and he was determined to set a record for quick passage. Before he left port, he searched every possible source for charts of the seas he was to navigate—down the eastern coast of South America, around treacherous Cape Horn, up the western shore—but there were no charts, no guideposts. One sailor was supposed to learn from older ones. Superstition, hearsay, and tradition filled the sailor's lore.

Maury decided to change all that. He would keep exact records of all waters he crossed, the winds, the weather, the rocks, so that other mariners could profit by his experience.

He "scaled rocks and crept around the corners of cliffs" to make "astronomical and trigonometrical observations" along the shores. He measured the enormous depths of the seas, and the temperature of the waters at various levels. He discovered rivers of one temperature flowing at right angles to rivers of another temperature—one rushing below the other far below the ocean's surface.

Maury was fired by the fact that New York City owed its growth to the thermometer that Benjamin Franklin lowered into the sea in the 1780s. Until then, Charleston, South

Carolina, had been the leading United States port. Sailors had avoided stormy waters off the New England coast by heading straight from Europe for the balmy waters off the South Carolina coast, then riding the Gulf Stream northward. When Franklin's study showed sailors how they could dip thermometers in the sea and mark the Gulf Stream as precisely as a highway marker, they could take their bearings easily and navigate the shortcut from Europe to New York.

"This discovery . . . shortened the passage from 60 to 30 days, and consequently changed the course of trade," Maury wrote. "Thus an impulse was given to the prosperity of New York; one enterprise begat another, until that city became the great commercial emporium and center of exchange of the new world. All these results are traceable to the use of the thermometer at sea."

Maury's thermometer helped mark the quickest way around South America. When he came back to Washington in 1834, he set himself a task: to put in book form all the information he had gathered about navigating South American waters.

Before he settled down with his notes, Maury had a date to keep in Fredericksburg. On July 15, 1834, in an old mansion where George Washington had once gone to school, he married Ann Herndon. In Fredericksburg, in a charming old house with a hospitable garden, Maury and his bride made their first home and he wrote his first book, *A New Theoretical and Practical Treatise on Navigation*, published in 1836.

Maury's book soon became a textbook for junior navy officers. President Andrew Jackson thought it important enough to entitle Maury to a promotion and reimbursement for cost of publication, but the secretary of the navy ignored the president's recommendations. As the book went through many printings and its fame spread, other navy officers looked coldly on the Tennessee officer who presumed to read into the vagaries of the sea a pattern that sailors could depend on.

Triumph and Disaster

The rainy night that a toppling stagecoach hurled Matthew Fontaine Maury into the mud and broke his leg sparkles timorously in sea history as a match's flicker. For if that accident—dislocating a knee and splintering a thigh bone—had not removed the young navy officer from sea duty forever, it is doubtful that he ever would have had time to undertake his massive probing of the seas.

It was an August night in 1839 when thirty-three-year-old Lieutenant Maury was sitting high atop an overloaded stagecoach, on his way from his old Tennessee home to New York to board his ship for another stretch of sea duty. He was just returning from a visit to his ailing father, Richard Maury, on his Williamson County farm, when the stagecoach slipped off the wet road near Somerset, Ohio, and overturned.

Maury was never to sail his own ship again. But the gigantic projects that he began while he was convalescing, the answers he found on ocean floor and windy sky, and the charts he published to lead sailors through the world's most treacherous waters blazed a new trail in scientific discovery.

A whale, to Maury, held more secrets of the seas than all of the United States Navy put together. He had rough whaling-boat captains so convinced of the value of his findings that hundreds of them joined in the round-the-world project of identifying every whale they saw—keeping an exact record of what type it was, where they saw it, what the temperature and depth of the waters were, what the contents of the whale's stomach were if they killed it.

The latter information helped Maury find out why whales congregated in one area of the ocean and avoided others, whether they deserted certain parts because the food they sought on the ocean floor was too deep for them to reach, whether the temperature of the waters influenced the food supply, and whether the heat of the water repelled the whale.

Out of it all, Maury was dredging up one fact from one ocean and another clue from another sea to fit together like pieces of a jigsaw puzzle to form a dazzling three-dimensional picture of the sea. He lifted the black waters to show what lay deep under their surfaces, and showed man how he could travel safely between mountains that shoot up from the ocean floor like needles to bare their points as islands.

"The bed of the Atlantic is a deep and narrow trough," he wrote. "The bottom of the sea is, like the land, diversified with hill and dale. Vast plains spread themselves out at unfathomable depths—plateaus, banks, shoals and sand-shifts on the floor of the ocean; and mountains rising from it more perpendicularly than they do on the land. . . ."

He looked on the globe as an awesome machine, endlessly bathing land and sky with rain and snow to keep plants growing and animal life thriving. "The sea serves as a sewer to the land, and a reservoir for the clouds," Maury wrote in one of his picturesque geographies that lifted the subject to the realms of poetry and philosophy. "The sea is the highway of the world."

He was intrigued with the idea that the whale's highways might point to man's highways, that the waters they sought were weather makers for the world. He saw something significant in the fact that "right whales" of the same type were found in the northern tips of the Atlantic and Pacific oceans, and there was no obvious way for them to get from one side to the other except to make the long loop down

around North and South America, crossing the equator
twice.

But Maury's studies showed that was impossible. "To
the right whale, the equator is as a wall of fire," he wrote.
"The animal is never found near it, seldom or never within
1,000 miles of it, on either side."

That left only one explanation: the whales were swimming through open water under the North Pole, in a region
that had formerly been considered land. "It is another link
in the chain of circumstantial evidence going to prove the
existence of the Northwest Passage," he wrote in 1853.

Numerous explorers, including Matthew C. Perry, bore
out his discovery. The submarine *Nautilus* took his whale
route a hundred years later. Adm. Richard Byrd, who headed
an expedition to the South Pole in 1927, said that Maury's
speculations on that area in 1860 influenced his undertaking.

But Maury's sifting of ooze from the ocean floors bore
most dramatic fruit in 1854, when he was able to inform
Cyrus Field not only that it was possible to tie America to
Europe with a cable, but also that he knew exactly where
and when to lay it.

The thought of instant communication across the Atlantic shook two continents. "Practical" businessmen said it
was impossible. Politicians feared international entangle-
ments. (Tennessee's "Lean Jimmy" Jones, then senator,
fought government use of the proposed transatlantic telegraphic service because he "did not want anything to do
with England or Englishmen.")

The moment millionaire Field thought of laying the cable
across the Atlantic, he wrote Lt. Matthew Fontaine Maury,
asking the advice of the world authority on oceanography.
By one of those dramatic coincidences of history, Maury had
just written a letter on the subject to the secretary of the

navy, on February 22, 1854, reporting that a survey of the North Atlantic floor had revealed a high plateau stretching from Newfoundland to Ireland.

Moreover, he said, the soft ooze on the floor of the plateau (never more than two miles below the surface) was a fine seashell mixture and would cushion the cables safely. "This plateau seems to have been placed there especially for the purpose of holding the wires of a Submarine Telegraph, and of keeping them out of harm's way," Maury had advised the navy.

When he gave the same information to Field, that settled the matter. Samuel F. B. Morse assured Field that the underwater cable would work. All that was left to do was find financial backing for the project. Americans were slow to put money in such a fantastic undertaking, but Field raised the funds in England.

Scientists wore their pencils down with calculations of the number of miles of cable it would take to lay across the ocean, allowing for slack and the rise and fall of the ocean floor. They figured the size of copper wires that would transmit telegraphic signals, and the thickness of layer upon layer of insulating material that would protect the wire from water, sharks' teeth, whales' "ponderous flukes and terrible jaws," and the mountainous pull of storm-tossed waters.

Investors were so eager to see the job under way that Field did not have time to test sample cables before manufacturing began. Finding a ship big enough to carry cable to reach across the ocean (twenty-five hundred miles of cable weighing a ton a mile) was impossible. The solution was to use two steamships, one American and one British, and share the weight between them. The plan was to cut the cable in two, refit both ships so they could coil the miles of cable in their holds, then pay it out as they moved slowly across the ocean.

The American ship was to start out from Ireland and drop her cable across the ocean floor toward America. The British ship, sailing alongside, would splice on her end of the cable in mid-ocean, and would continue to the North American shore, at Newfoundland.

Maury told them they would find the quietest seas in July, but it was August 6, 1857, before they got started. Not five miles out, the cable broke, and they had to go back, lift the cable, and repair it.

For the next three days, London was agog at telegraphic messages that came from the ship. Far beyond the shallows now, they were easing the cable over the side of the ship "to the awful depth of 2,000 fathoms."

"Still the iron cord buried itself in the waves, and every instant the flash of light in the darkened telegraph room told of the passage of the electric current," a London telegrapher reported.

But on the fourth day out, with 335 miles of cable on the ocean floor, it snapped in two when brakes on the paying-out machine were applied. There was not enough cable left for a new try, and the season was too late for manufacturing more. There was nothing to do but try again the next year.

On June 10, 1858, the second of three heartbreaking attempts began. This time the two ships would sail to mid-ocean together, splice the cable there, and sail to opposite shores, dropping cable as they went.

Two days after they sailed from Plymouth, the two heavy ships and the two ships escorting them ran into a fierce storm and were scattered in all directions. It was considered miraculous that the heavily weighted ships managed to survive the wild waves, and equally miraculous that when the storm faded, all four ships met in a calm sea, at the very spot where the cables were to be spliced.

On June 26, linked to each other by their spliced cables, the two ships sailed off toward opposite shores. They had gone three miles when the cable tangled in the paying-out machine and the line broke. In constant telegraphic touch with each other, the ships turned back to repair the damage. They were eighty miles apart when it broke again, and they turned back to splice a new cable. They were two hundred miles apart when the cable broke the third time. By then the food supply was so low that they had to return to Plymouth.

By July 29 they were back in the mid-Atlantic for another try. This time the American ship, the *Niagara*, sailed toward America in ideal weather, slowly unwinding 1,030 miles of cable to the bottom of the ocean. On shore in Newfoundland, the cable was spliced to a telegraph line that went to New York.

But the British ship, the *Agamemnon*, sailing from mid-ocean to Ireland, ran into one crisis after another. First a whale made straight for the trailing cable, "at a great speed, rolling and tossing the sea into foam all around." At the last moment, the "ponderous living mass" missed ship and cable, "just grazing the cable where it entered the water."

That scare was hardly passed when telegraphers, mathematicians, and other scientists on board "shook like an aspen leaf" when all communication between the two ships stopped. Nobody ever knew what happened, but after an hour and a half of silence, the signals began again.

Scientists and crew had hardly recovered from that near catastrophe when a storm bore down on them so fiercely that the cable dangled on towering waves above the ship like a silvery thread. The ship had to move at a set speed to keep the cable moving properly, and the fuel supply ran short. But the storm finally blew itself out, with the cable still intact.

The ship was nearly in sight of the Irish shore when the

last threat came. An American ship innocent of the *Agamem-non*'s task came close and was about to cut across the cable. The escorting ship had to fire her guns to scare the Americans away.

On Thursday, August 5, the English ship touched land and brought in her end of the cable. She had hardly landed when the message came over the cable that the American ship had reached Newfoundland. Together the two ships had laid 2,350 miles of cable across the Atlantic, and at both ends of the line people were swept up in a great frenzy of excitement.

Celebrators in New York set the roof of the city hall on fire with fireworks. The stolid *Times* of London rhapsodized: "The Atlantic is dried up, and we become in reality as well as in wish one country."

American preachers quoted Psalms to celebrate the event: "Their line is gone out through all the earth, and their words to the end of the world."

Queen Victoria sent a message over the marvelous new metal rope to President Buchanan. She knighted a British scientist for his part in the project, and New Yorkers feted Cyrus Field, the man who had kept at the project when all others despaired.

The first news story came over the wires on August 27, 1858, but the signals were already growing weaker. On September 1, less than a month after the cables were laid, the last message sputtered through. The insulation had failed. From then on, all was silence. The years of work, tons of cable, and millions of dollars spent on the project had vanished in the soft white ooze of the Atlantic's floor.

The public was outraged. Newspapers speculated on whether the whole thing had been a hoax to lure investors. It would be eight years before money could be raised for a new and successful cable.

Long before that, civil war had split our nation and Maury had resigned his commission in the U.S. Navy to defend the Confederacy. He was deprived of any part in the final cable effort, and only Maximilian of Mexico remembered in 1866 to decorate Maury for his "illustrious labors . . . in laying the Transatlantic Cable . . . uniting both hemispheres."

At Last, Hurrahs for the Sailor

Clouds were lifting somewhat the May day in 1868 that Matthew Fontaine Maury, a stocky hero in red silk cowl, stood before a British audience to receive Cambridge's highest honors. The Tennessee scientist, bald and badgered with hardship, had been so stripped of honor in his homeland that he could hardly conceal his pride in the new tribute from the English university.

"So you don't know what I mean by the 'coronation'?" he wrote a friend. "Why boy, I'm a Cambridge LL.D. and am going there—I and Max and the Queen on the 28th—she to unveil the Prince Consort and I to be rigged up in 'dyed garments from Bozra' in a gown and a cap and a beautiful red silk cowl and hear myself all done up in Latin!"

In Latin, the dean paid tribute to Maury's "attentive observations of the course of the winds, the climate, the currents of the seas and oceans . . . which.are now in the hands of all seamen . . . and have carried the fame of the author into the most distant countries of the earth."

Two British celebrities also received honorary degrees from the university that day, and one of them wrote Maury later: "Lord, what a figure we three of us looked, dressed up like lobsters, in the midst of that big hall, gazed at by such a host of people. . . ."

But Maury, who had been so popular with American

audiences nine years before that he was mentioned for the presidency, was a veteran of lecture tours. His speeches on the wonders of the sea and its influence on every person's crops and business had kept him before enthralled audiences for years before the Civil War.

From the time, almost thirty years before, that the stagecoach accident had sent him to his Fredericksburg, Virginia, home for a long and painful recovery under the care of his devoted wife, he had turned to research. "Make it a rule to make everything bend to your profession," he told his eight children, and he set an example by using his convalescence to write magazine articles exposing the problems of the navy.

He advocated complete reorganization of the navy, establishment of a navy academy, and development of inland waterways, particularly in the South. Congress put most of his suggestions in force. He pulled hard for a navy station at Memphis and a navy base at Pensacola. His powerful pen brought him, three years after his accident, the most significant appointment of his career: director of the U.S. Naval Observatory in Washington.

It was Maury who shaped the observatory into its influential role as a research center, both in astronomy and on the seas. He moved his family to Washington and established them in the new residence built onto one wing of the observatory. There, for years, he hardly divided working hours from private life. He was constantly absorbed in his papers, his charts, his maps. His children climbed over his knees as he wrote.

Since his early days at sea, Maury had been shocked at the navy's haphazard approach to navigation. If it were not for the British almanac, he said in disgust, American ships could hardly find their way home.

Maury drew charts that blocked the oceans' surfaces off

in small squares, and appealed to seamen on all ships to make a precise record of every condition of sea and air in every square they passed through. Out of that mass of material, he hoped to "blaze a way through the winds of the sea by which the navigator may find the best paths at all seasons."

Old sailors were skeptical. At first they ignored his appeals. He had to dig through discarded log books of the navy for most of the data in his first "Wind and Current Chart of the North Atlantic," published in 1847.

Maury predicted that the chart would cut sailing time from the usual fifty-five days to forty or forty-five on the New York to Rio run. One of the first ships to follow Maury's directions made it in thirty-five days, and other seamen pricked up their ears.

By the end of 1848, captains in all oceans eagerly sought his charts, in return for which they promised to keep their own full records to send along to him. Suddenly old sea captains were grappling the ocean floor for information like pirates after gold. "You will never find a Captain who goes into the thing as heartily as Captain Platt does," one young navy lieutenant boasted as his ship sounded the depths of the Mediterranean.

Testing the lines—of waxed twine or silk or wire—to find one that would not snap under the pull of fierce undercurrents and bucking seas was a maddening process. "It really appeared as if some monster of the deep had hold of the weight below and was walking off with it," one awed captain wrote of currents rushing deep under the surface.

In calm seas, soundings were difficult enough, but they were impossible "with a smashing breeze and a large sea on." Even with calm surface waters, the lines (with thirty-two-pound weights trailing the ocean floor) often snapped under the pull of undercurrents.

"While the shot remained on the bottom, I could draw it along with my naked hand," one Captain Barron reported to Maury. "But so soon as it lifted, I could not move it with a glove on, the weight was so great, and the pain in my hand so severe. One of our quartermasters, as strong a man as we have aboard, could not raise the shot an inch, at 2,000 fathoms depth."

It was obvious to Maury that some of the soundings were inaccurate. The weighted lines, instead of dropping straight to the ocean floor or even trailing out at a calculated angle, were drawn out "in the shape of a loop" by tugging crosscurrents.

To make comparisons reliable, Maury had the ships make their soundings with the same kind of twine, treated in the same way, and with the same size weights. He called on ships' crews to drop bottles overboard, "carefully corked and sealed and thrown overboard at noon," with "slips of paper, giving name and position of ship, etc." inside.

Out of it all, Maury calculated ocean currents and speeds, the "roof top" of the warm Gulf Stream that rose in a ridge and let no wreckage or bottle cross to the other side, and the influence of water currents on wind and weather across the lands. The information he prepared for sailing boats paved the way for air navigation a century later.

He asked his "floating laboratories" to be sure to save "specimens of the ooze (a piece as large as a pea will be ample)" that might cling to the anchor as it was lifted from the ocean floor. "I will esteem it as a favor if you will have them procured—properly and carefully labeled—and sent me," he instructed sea captains from the China Sea to the South Pacific, from the Dead Sea to the Arctic.

He asked for samples of water from the various oceans, at varying depths, to test for saltiness and plant and animal life. He yearned to ascend into "upper regions of the atmosphere" to prove his theories on air currents.

"I set out with no theory, and I have none to build up," he stated. "I set out with the view of collecting facts."

Maury tried to get at least a hundred observations for every month, in every small section of the sea. However, he admitted, there were portions of the sea where he had eighteen hundred observations a month, and others where he did well to get one.

When the Gold Rush of 1849 turned California into a Promised Land and shippers joined the stampede to rush men and supplies from the East Coast, Maury's charts got their first big test. It was half a year's journey, 180 days, to travel by boat from New York to San Francisco then. Maury's charts soon cut almost seven weeks off the trip, making it possible in 133 days.

Suddenly the eyes of the world were on the fifteen-thousand-mile route around the southern tip of South America. It became the "race course of the oceans," and clippers set their sails to break all records. When some of the clippers using Maury's charts cut the trip down to 110 days, the public was astounded. In 1851, when the *Flying Cloud* "fairly flew" around the course in 89 days and 21 hours, headlines shouted and readers gasped. That was half the old pre-Maury time. Easterners who had settled in San Francisco felt they were close to home now. San Franciscans celebrated the sailing riotously.

Maury, the quiet, plodding researcher, was suddenly hero of the day. New York shippers embarrassed the navy lieutenant with a gift of five thousand dollars cash and a fine silver service. American universities heaped honorary degrees on him, ships were named for him, and statues in foreign ports were unveiled and medals struck in his honor by foreign governments.

The czar of Russia, the king of Denmark, the emperor of France, and the king of Portugal appointed him to their highest orders. Norway and Sweden, Prussia, Holland, Austria, and Sardinia saluted him as one of the great scientists of all time.

Eighteen nations responded quickly when he called a "summit conference" in Belgium in August, 1853, so shippers in all lands could coordinate plans to map every mile of the seas. He was pleading not only for a "universal plan of observations at sea," but also for a system of weather records to be kept on land, throughout the world. However, ship owners and underwriters were quicker to see the value than farmers and politicians, and land observations were postponed.

But shippers from Denmark, France, England, the Netherlands, Norway, Portugal, Russia, and Sweden joined quickly with the United States in carrying out Maury's sea plans. Shortly afterward, eight other countries joined their fleets to his "floating laboratories."

"Rarely before has there been such a sublime spectacle presented to the scientific world," Maury wrote when the conference ended on September 8, 1853. "All nations agree to unite . . . in carrying out one system of philosophical research with regard to the sea. Though they may be enemies in all else, here they are to be friends. Every ship that navigates the high seas, with these charts and abstract logs on board, may henceforth be regarded as a floating observatory."

Jubilant mariners reported that new charts cut sailing time from New York to Rio by one-fourth. But jealous officers in the U.S. Navy determined to cut Maury down. First, they saw to it that he received no promotion. Then, when Congress sought to reward him with twenty-five thousand dollars "as some substantial evidence of the appreciation of the benefits he has, by his labors, conferred upon his country," his fellow officers blocked the action.

Even that was not enough. In one of the disgraceful plots of history, a spitefully assembled navy board decided in September, 1855, to demote Maury, cut his pay to twelve hundred dollars a year, and place him on inactive duty "because of his old leg injury"—a blow almost beyond Maury's comprehension. The gentle scholar, a rigidly honest man who spent all his nonworking hours with a family that adored him, could hardly believe that men could stoop so low.

He quietly set about getting the facts before the proper authority. After constant rebuffs, he managed to get his cause before the U.S. Senate, and it was championed by newspapers over the country.

At last, in January, 1858, after three years of conniving on the part of scores of jealous navy officers, restitution was made. The president not only restored Maury to active service in the navy, but promoted him to commander.

Trouble for Commander Maury was just beginning. He had concerned himself for years with fair and peaceful settlement of the slavery question. He hoped for a means that would resettle the slaves in other lands, yet not strip the South of its "$1,500-million" investment. But once the war had begun, Maury saw only one course: to cut every tie with the U.S. Navy, with his beloved research labs at the observatory, with the U.S. government, and to defend his homeland, the South.

On April 20, 1861, the day his resignation as director of the observatory was effective, he worked hard to the last hour. That afternoon at three o'clock, when he turned his prized records over to the next officer in rank and left the building forever, Maury was in tears.

"Its associations, the treasures there, which had been collected from the sea, were precious to me," he wrote, "and as I turned my back upon the place, I could not but recollect that such things were."

He immediately moved his family to Fredericksburg, Virginia, and when the secretary of the navy asked the reasons for the resignation, Maury replied: "They are these: our glorious Union is gone; the state through which and for which I confessed allegiance to the Federal government has no longer any lot or part in it. Neither have I. I desire to go with my own people and with them to share the fortunes of our own state together."

Maury had no idea how rough the going would be. Navy officers who had always resented his fame now denounced his volumes of *Sailing Directions* as "unsound, with little that is practically useful." They issued instructions that they "no longer be issued in their present form." They banished his name from history books, and succeeded so well that only in the United States is his name practically unknown. They trumped up charges of "treason" against him.

Even in the Confederate navy, Maury was plagued by bickering officers, lack of funds, lack of equipment. He was put to research, and developed explosive "torpedoes" to plant along southern coasts to destroy invaders. "This is a business, this thing of blowing up men while they are asleep, that I don't glory in," Maury wrote. "I shall endeavor to . . . save the crews from drowning." Though he did not originate the idea, Maury is credited with being the first to make "electrical torpedoes successfully used against an enemy in war."

He turned down handsome offers from other countries that wanted to set him up in laboratories to continue his research, but did accept a "special assignment" in London from the Confederate secretary of the navy. In his job as purchasing agent for the Confederacy, he was caught in Cuba at the end of the war. After a dramatic stay in Mexico, he returned to England, and his family joined him there in 1866.

European governments engaged him for lectures and honored him with cash gifts and honorary degrees. It was in 1868 that Cambridge gave him an honorary degree, and Maury used the occasion to plead for British support for a new college in Tennessee, the University of the South at Sewanee.

Maury was invited to become head of the new university, and was offered similar jobs at the University of Tennessee and the University of Alabama. He accepted a job on the faculty of Virginia Military Institute, and Robert E. Lee was among the old friends who welcomed him and his family to Lexington that fall.

"Here we are in our new home, busy fixing up," he wrote happily after years of war and wandering. "And things begin to know their places. . . . People are very kind, the country is beautiful, the scenery is lovely."

He set to the job of revising old textbooks and writing new ones, and spoke in behalf of nationwide weather observation. In the fall of 1872, while he was on a speaking tour that reached from Boston to Saint Louis, the sixty-six-year-old Maury fell ill.

"Are my feet cold? Do I drag my anchors?" the dying sailor asked his family, gathered around his bed in their Lexington, Virginia, home on February 1, 1873. "All is well."

The flags of Tennessee and Virginia hung in the college chapel where final services were held. Tennessee had a portrait of him painted in its capitol ceiling, and a bust of him in the hall. But all the world follows his "footprints in the sea." Every weather report, every cablegram, every broadcast from abroad, every ship, and every plane in its flight sings of the work of the Tennessee boy who went to sea so long ago.

"There is no one living in the United States or in any civilized country whose daily life is not affected through the scientific researches of this man," one historian wrote. "He was truly the 'Pathfinder of the Seas.'"

Capt. William Driver
and the Flag

Seven ships sailed out of Salem that frozen January 13, 1831, and all but one were lost. That was the two-masted brig commanded by Capt. William Driver, who lived in Nashville, Tennessee, most of his life and whose bones rest in the old City Cemetery under a tombstone he designed himself.

The log of that fantastic voyage that began in a sheet of ice and ended in tropic adventure was acquired in 1967 by the manuscript division of the Tennessee State Library and Archives. In his own fine hand, on salt-sprayed pages, Driver recorded two great stories not generally known before.

One is of that ghostly storm off the New England coast. The other is of his rescue of the "poor, pitiful sad People of Pitcairn"—the survivors and children of those who had committed the famous mutiny of the *Bounty*. Driver was convinced the rest of his life that God had spared him from the first ordeal for the second task.

Captain Driver was twenty-seven years old the winter day in 1831 when he faced the fiercest storm of his life. He had been sailing the seas for over thirteen years, and knew most of the ports of Europe and the Orient. His career began, he said, when he was thirteen and a half years old—small for his age and apprenticed to a blacksmith.

"I was so small that I had to stand on an empty candle box to reach my arms over the bellows pole," he wrote. "One Sunday the smith's wife put me in a brown muslin shirt with a ruffled bosom and hurried me off to Sunday School."

That was too much for young William. He ripped the ruffles off his shirt, and in high indignation, rushed down to the pier where one of the biggest, swiftest ships of its day, the *China*, was about to set sail for a trip around the world. Just as they were weighing anchor, Driver climbed aboard and signed on as cabin boy.

The story goes that the runaway boy got word from his father not to return home until he was captain of his own ship. Seven years later, he was.

In the margin of one of his books, Driver wrote that he was paid "28 Spanish dollars" for his services at the end of that first voyage, and the ship's owner told him that was for "being the smartest boy that ever went to sea."

"That made me what I was and what I am," the old sea captain reminisced at eighty.

In foreign ports, on the *China*, he learned what it meant to have a United States flag flying high, to feel the protection of our government under that banner. When, at age twenty-one, he qualified as master mariner and was licensed to sail a ship, he received the most cherished gift of his lifetime. His mother and the "girls of Salem," the Massachusetts port town where he was born and grew up, had made him a flag to fly on his ship.

They gave it to him on his birthday, March 17, and every Saint Patrick's Day for the rest of his life (as well as July 4 and Washington's birthday), he flew that same flag, even in his later years in Nashville. It was a giant, sturdy flag, measuring twelve by twenty-four feet, and on the day he had it hoisted on the first ship under his command, the thrill was unspeakable. "I'll call her 'Old Glory,' boys!" he shouted, and he never again referred to the flag in any other way.

It was several voyages and six years later when he ran

the flag up on the *Charles Doggett* to set sail for the South Pacific. That wintry day in 1831 had started out bright and clear, and Captain Driver watched six ships of "various riggs" sail away from Salem, all taking the narrow South Channel. Before the day was gone, all six ships would be lost, and all the crews except one.

But Captain Driver—a short, muscular man with dark hair and gray eyes—knew the traps along the treacherous coast. He watched a leaden patch grow wider in the sky and knew he had to get his ship out of harbor—fast. It was loaded with six hundred kegs of gunpowder. Young Captain Driver was sure a snowstorm was about to blow in. He left word at the harbor for his friends not to worry: he would take the safer East Channel out.

"That saved our brig and lives," he said later.

By seven o'clock that night, as Driver's ship passed a lighthouse twelve miles out, the wind was "due north and rapidly increasing, with a thick ragged scudd; weather very cold, brig making ice very fast—my men suffering dreadfully...."

Driver sent all the men he could spare into the cabin and "set up a small stove for their comfort when off duty"— an act of kindness he was to regret. All night the men on deck struggled desperately with the ice-loaded sails, trying to adjust them without splitting the canvas in the howling wind. Driver ached for them.

"Our poor men, just out from home and fireside, miserably clothed," he wrote. "My God, how they were suffering! And what a night! Dark as the Ages of Chaos. A high irregular sea, our poor little Brig rising like some mad Fury from the dark sea trough, shaking the white foam from her bow to plunge and rise again more madly if possible."

No longer could they control the wind-filled, frozen sails.

"We were running free," Driver continued the tale of sea-borne horror.

The straining ship creaked and groaned. "A voice at my side (Mr. Goodhue) said, 'Sir, she can't stand it.'"

Driver answered that there was nothing to do but fight the wind, which was driving them straight toward deadly shoals. "Better founder here without a stick standing than bury our bones on that fatal sand," he told Goodhue.

"So we tore away 'full and by' under our three fore and after sails, heading East to E.N. East, about four and one-half knots. It now began to snow. Sent all hands in the cabin but helmsman, with second mate in companionway, and myself at Weather Wheel. It was blowing a tornado. We done all we could. Our sails were all new." But if any change in sails had to be made, "we were helpless," Driver said.

"Our Brig was a block of ice; the forward deck ankle-deep with slush; again and again swept by the sea comb which was thrown up by the fury of the storm—a perfect cloud of sea-spray drift. Brother, could you have stood there, on that groaning deck, as we did, helpless, and alone with God, you would be able to realize a scene which no pen can describe. You would have felt the cold breath from the Chasm of Death. Could you have seen the despairing look of those poor seamen as they scanned your face for any cheering look, you would have found strength sufficient for the hour, for you would have felt *God is here also. I will trust him and save these poor fellows if our brig holds together.*"

"Day came at last, and showed a muddy, greenish yellow water all around us, and a wild confused sea," he wrote. "Saw the Schooner *Madison* standing in on her starboard tack, a fatal mistake—for she was lost and all on board."

Sounding the shallow depths, Driver found that "any less water and we were gone." But the wind suddenly shifted, and he had his men beat the sails clear of ice "with heavers and handspikes," and finally got the whole foresail up without splitting.

"Once well set, the sails drove us through the white foam like a wild sea gull," he wrote.

They were running through the sea at eight knots, and Driver said he could not have navigated through the deadly shallows at that rate but for the heavy, damp snowfall that seemed to break the sea.

"At this time I had a man at the wheel named Smith—a tall, lean picture of misfortune, who had been shipwrecked on his two preceding voyages," Driver wrote. "No wonder he seemed to tremble, and occasionally made remarks instigated by fear."

Fear was catching, and Driver felt the contagion. He sent Smith inside, and called "a little Dutchman named Francis" to take Smith's place. "I gave him my Rubber Boots, placed him at the Lee Wheel, and took the Weather Wheel myself, ordering him not to speak out loud no matter what he heard or seen. I should hear or see as quick as he did."

Driver sent all hands below, leaving only himself and the little Dutchman to fight the storm.

"There on deck we two stood silent and freezing until 5 P.M., when smoking water, ice all gone, etc., told us we were safe on inner edge of gulf stream." The winds abated during the night, "and early next day we were away on our voyage to New Zealand and Tahiti."

There were tolls from the storm. Once when Driver went to the cabin to warm his hands, he found the "stove full of fire had capsized during the fearful struggle, with only a two-inch plank between it and 600 kegs of powder." He had it "pitched overboard in no time," and that was "the first and last of that family I ever allowed on board ship, cold or no cold."

It was the custom then for ships to carry livestock to supply fresh meat for long voyages, but "all our livestock perished in the gale except a large mastiff, 'Charley,' and an old Red Rooster stowed in the cuddy of our surf boats on deck. And as day came, he would crow mightily in spite of the storm. This was very cheering to all."

There were other storms on that voyage, and calms that lasted for days under a beating sun. There was a fog for forty days. There were flying fish and the perilous passage around Cape Horn, and Driver's first glimpse of "Southern Lights—a clashing and mingling confusion together, a very picture of the Aurora Borealis." There were "high and heady" trade winds and fine weather and the cry "Sail ho!" from aloft. "Passed and was hailed by a Double Decker ship," he wrote on Sunday, February 20.

Driver reached New Zealand on Sunday, June 5, 1831— 120 days after he sailed from Salem. But his welcome there was hardly what he would have chosen. He had barely dropped anchor when natives, men and women, swarmed over the sides of the ship.

The women lavished their attentions on the sailors while the native men stole. Driver said he didn't know how he would have got rid of them if he had not had "our mastiff dog Charley" to chase them overboard. "When turned loose, he cleared the Deck in a Jiffie, taring some of the creatures badly."

Because it was Sunday, Driver "positively refused" to trade with any of the "huge lot who thronged on deck." Far from running away from Sunday school now, the captain was strict about holding religious services aboard ship on the Sabbath, and he allowed no carousing on board at any time. Having a wife and four-year-old son back home in Salem, he was outraged to see sailors, married as well as unmarried, welcome the attentions of native women.

"I spent the day unpleasantly, being debarred of our usual devotions by a throng on whom the Light of the Gospel had hardly dawned." And he was disgusted with the "unworthy throng of sailors from different Nations who have left the ship to spend their lives wallowing in Vices which even a savage must despise."

Three weeks later, on June 24, he left New Zealand, and it was "the latter part of July" when he anchored at balmy Tahiti, the land of beautiful women and palm-shaded languor. The adventure that began there would make his name known around the world.

A Favor for the Queen of Tahiti

The queen of the Tahitians, young and beautiful, came to Capt. William Driver to ask a favor. It was late in July, 1831, and he had hardly dropped anchor in the palm-fringed bay where a tropic breeze was blowing and spicy blossoms scented the air. Young Captain Driver dutifully noted in his ship's log that the young women accompanying the queen had "fine forms, pleasing features, smooth skins and brimming eyes." Their silky black hair fell over bare waists, and their smiles showed fine white teeth.

The favor the queen wanted was not a simple one. On her island, at that very moment, were the Polynesian wives and half-breed children of the British sailors who had mutinied on the *Bounty* forty-two years before.

For more than forty years the mutineers and their wives and offspring had shut themselves away from the world on a distant isle. In those years that had begun in bloodshed and terror, they had changed into sin-conscious Christians who found the loose morals and scanty clothing of the Polynesians intolerable.

When a drought threatened them with starvation six

months earlier, the queen told Driver, she had welcomed these hungry people to Tahiti's shores. But they had turned out to be a long-faced lot, threatening the happiness of her own subjects. Would Captain Driver take these people aboard his ship and return them to their own island—Pitcairn?

Pitcairn! The island famous around the world as refuge of the men who had mutinied on the *Bounty*. Every sailor knew the story of that mutiny and the trial that followed. They argued through long watches whether the sensitive Lt. Fletcher Christian and his followers had been justified in rebelling against the cruelties of the bullying Captain Bligh by sending him away from his own ship in a small boat.

All of that had happened long ago, fourteen years before Driver was born. He had grown up in a New England port town hearing the tale. Now here he was at Tahiti, weighing the future of all that was left of the mutineers. What he decided, and why, is recorded in Driver's own hand in his log books.

Driver could think of many good reasons for saying no to Queen Pomare. His ship, the brigantine *Charles Doggett*, was not equipped to carry sixty-five passengers. Even if it had been, Driver would be risking his career by making the voyage, which would take him fourteen hundred miles off his prescribed course. His insurance on both ship and cargo would be forfeited if he deviated from "projected voyages." If the slightest accident occurred, he would be "a ruined man at 27."

Then something happened that changed his mind: the queen took him to see the Pitcairn people.

Driver was stunned. "Poor sickly-looking despondent creatures, huddled together in a large thatch house where 12 of their number had died of Typhoid or Ship Fever!" he reported. Among the dead was "the flower of their flock," Fletcher Christian's son, the handsome Thursday October Christian, firstborn of Pitcairn.

The women, in ragged dresses that reached to the ground, were dirty; the men, in baggy trousers, were cowed and hungry. Queen Pomare had called them "poor crying children." They were despondent, too, at the "free and easy ways" of the Tahitians. Driver himself described Queen Pomare and her Tahitians as "creatures of tropical passion."

"No restraints thrown around them in Youth, they indulged in every desire and cared not who fell as long as their fall gratified a personal appetite," Driver wrote. The Tahitians, a happy people who spent their days swimming and surf riding, had taunted the Pitcairn people about their long dresses and pious prayers and hymns.

Captain Driver said the Pitcairn people told him "time and again" of that "horrid day" when they arrived at Tahiti to witness the "depravity" of the people of this "brink of Pollution." They were afraid their own young people would come to like the "voluptuous life."

"Fearful and jealous of all around them, they became careless, indolent and dirty," Driver said. "They huddled together in a miserable thatched Bowery, a building used for Tahitian festivals. . . . Here disease found them and swept away one-sixth of their number. . . . Sad, helpless little flock! They came to me with all their sorrows, begging to be taken home, offering to sell or give all they possessed if I would take them." They had rather die on Pitcairn, they said, than live at Tahiti.

Driver, the stern New England churchman, saw his duty. He had to rescue these Christians from the loose morality of the Polynesians. He was convinced now that this was the purpose for which "God spared us in that dread storm when six other vessels perished with their crews."

So on August 14, 1831, seven months after he sailed out of Salem in that fierce winter storm, Captain Driver loaded his ship at Tahiti with "65 helpless creatures—mostly women and children" for the voyage to Pitcairn.

"If ever Joy was depicted on any face, it was on the Pitcairn people as I hoisted sail and pulled away for that home from which they had been absent about six months," he wrote.

That load, plus all their possessions and provisions for the three-week voyage, and the ship's crew of eighteen, taxed the two-masted brig to capacity. Driver was aware that they were facing "one of the most dangerous seas known—the Ocean of Coral Reefs, of islands dotted here and there—all this and more." He had no extra linen aboard for passengers. He himself slept on deck throughout the voyage, and the first night out a baby was born.

"We trusted God," Driver wrote. "He blessed us with mild, beautiful weather the entire trip of 21 days. We never closed our hatchway nor had one case of sickness."

Captain Driver lectured the people on their treatment of poor, trusting Mary Christian, "the most downcast creature I ever met with." Mary had been victim of a visiting British seaman, and she and the resulting illegitimate child were "left alone, shunned."

"It was part of my agreement with the Pitcairn people that she should be forgiven, as they were guilty of allowing a stranger among such innocent girls," Driver said. "I insisted on her forgiveness and reinstatement in society. This has been done. She wept for joy."

Captain Driver divided work among his passengers. The men did the cooking; the women cared for the children. The families took turns cooking—one family doing all of the cooking for all the passengers for one day. Driver worried because they ate only vegetables and fruit.

He talked with them about what had happened to the
mutineers after they put Captain Bligh off the *Bounty*. All
nine of the mutineers were dead now—the last, John
Adams, had died two years before. Their descendants told
Driver how the mutineers had zig-zagged across the South
Pacific in the *Bounty* for nine months before they saw
Pitcairn at sunset one day—the uninhabited island they
sought as a hiding place.

Pitcairn was a sharp needle of an island protected by long
coral reefs that would scrape the bottom off prying ships.
When Fletcher Christian and his band of mutineers scaled the
rocky shaft, they found a "little Garden of Eden." The fertile
top dimpled into a little valley and rose in sheltering hills
around the rim.

The weather was balmy the year round, and there on the
island covering two square miles grew melons, bananas, yams,
coconuts, oranges, and the large-leafed tree from which
people wove their clothes and thatched their roofs. Christian
had brought along chickens, pigs, and goats. He stripped
every tool and scrap of material he could use from the ship,
and on January 27, 1790, burned the hulk and sank it. His
tracks, he felt, were forever covered.

But trouble arose because of the Tahitian women
Christian had brought along for himself, his fellow mutineers,
and the six Tahitian men who came along to help with culti-
vating the crops. The twenty-eight people who came to the
island had been there only three years when the Tahitian men
plotted to kill the white men and take their wives. Fletcher
Christian, leader of the little colony, was the first victim—shot
from ambush as he worked in his garden.

The whites retaliated. When it was over, the only men left
alive were two Englishmen: Alexander Smith (later known as
John Adams) and Edward Young. These two, suddenly aware

of what jealousy and greed had done to their "Garden of Eden," resolved to reform. They got out their Bible and prayer book and began reading and teaching.

They set up a school for the women and children with the Bible the chief textbook. They had the whole community gather in school for morning and evening prayer services every day, and for five services on Sunday. Young soon died, but Smith lived nearly thirty years longer as teacher, preacher, "father" to the little tribe.

The Pitcairn people told Captain Driver that it was twenty years before a ship discovered their hiding place. By that time, England was too involved in war with France to bother with trying Smith, the lone survivor.

Driver said he found the Pitcairn style of speaking English "a little droll." And he, like the various British officers who had visited Pitcairn, was amazed at the innocence of these people who quoted Milton and the Bible and spent their days in a dreamlike blend of religious ardor and tropic ease.

When a severe drought struck the island in 1830, a British ship rescued the colony from starvation, moving them to Tahiti. There, six months later, Captain Driver had found them.

They would never forget his kindness in taking them back to Pitcairn, they told him. But the mood of the homecoming was somber. "At the cry of 'Leand O!' some might be seen weeping over the clothing of all that remained of their dear departed friends," Driver wrote. "Some were pacing the deck, slowly and sad. Very few willing to give way to joy. Poor fellows, as we neared the Land, a silent sorrow seemed to prevail."

On Sunday, September 4, 1831, Driver finished landing the Pitcairn people on their craggy island. They were shutting themselves off from the world forever, they felt. They wrote a formal note of thanks and presented it as he departed, stating that "Capt. Driver behaved with the greatest kindness and humanity becoming a man and a Christian."

As his ship sailed away, he heard them call out, "God bless you! We will write your name upon our walls!"

Driver was still a young man when he gave up the sea in 1837, just six years after his rescue of the Pitcairn people. That was when his wife, Martha, died and left him with three young children, one a baby. Driver had two brothers, Henry and John, who had gone to Nashville eleven years earlier, and he moved to the southern city to be near them.

His brother Henry's wife had a pretty niece, Mary Jane Parks, just fifteen years old at the time. A few weeks after he arrived in Nashville, the thirty-five-year-old Captain Driver married Mary Jane at Christ Episcopal Church, where he was a devoted member the rest of his life. There he and Mary Jane were confirmed, there their nine children were baptized, there "Captain Billy" served as vestryman and junior warden, and there he and some of his friends tried to form a new congregation. When he and Mary Jane brought their youngest to the church to be baptized, the name they chose commemorated the "greatest adventure of my life," Driver said. They named the child Thomas Pitcairn.

Captain Driver worked in Nashville as salesman for various business establishments, including his brothers' store. He maintained his Yankee sympathies throughout the Civil War.

Nashvillians had become accustomed to seeing Captain Driver's huge old flag, the one the "Salem girls" had made for him to fly on his ships around the world. Every holiday and election day, he displayed it on a rope stretched from an upstairs window of his home to a tree across the street. During the Civil War, he hid the flag, sewing it in a quilt for safekeeping. He wrote letters to editors of Northern newspapers, never failing to mention "Old Glory." The name caught on, and Driver himself was nicknamed "Old Glory Driver."

To his great sorrow, three of his sons served in the Confederate army, and one died of battle wounds. But it was Driver's great ship's flag that rose over the state capitol when Nashville fell to the Union army.

During Federal occupation, he was a city councilman and ran unsuccessfully for mayor. He served on the Union-appointed commission to hear claims against the Federal government for property damage done by Federal troops in Nashville. One interesting sidelight: he became a violent enemy of the Union-appointed military governor of Tennessee, Andrew Johnson.

When Driver was an old man, he sat in the parlor of his South Nashville home and entertained grandchildren with stories of his adventures on the voyage to Pitcairn. "It was one of the greatest occurrences of my life," he wrote a few years before his death, at age eighty-three, in Nashville on March 3, 1886. "If I ever knew the pleasure of blessing others, and being thereby blessed, it was when I saw this people safe on their native shores."

When he designed his tombstone, he left instructions that his rescue of the Pitcairn people be inscribed thereon. And so it was, near the anchor on his monument in old City Cemetery in Nashville.

Steamboatin' Tom Ryman

Hero of the nation's steamboating days might have been Tom Ryman, not Tom Sawyer, if Mark Twain had lived in Tennessee. For young Tom Ryman, who knew the water like his own skin, ran his own commercial fishing boats on the Tennessee and the Cumberland when he was seventeen and dreamed then of someday operating his own steamboat line.

Born in Nashville in 1841, when steamboating was just beginning, Ryman rode the crest through the steamboat's most powerful days in the 1870s, and was the mightiest fighter on the Cumberland against railroad competition until he died early this century. Ryman, a tall, lean, quiet man—gentle with the suffering, shrewd in business—finally owned and operated the most powerful fleet of steamboats on the rip-roaring, cotton-shipping Cumberland of a century ago.

He was hero to hundreds of river men before he ever "got religion" and built a gigantic auditorium to share it. His ingenuity and skill in rescuing his boats from rapids and shoals, from wild floodwaters and snagging trees, were the boast of "bettin' men" in saloons all up and down the Cumberland, the Tennessee, and the Ohio.

Myths about the man whose name lived on in the Ryman Auditorium for generations (until it became the Opry House) have blacked out the true story of Capt. Tom Ryman. But now the memoirs of his daughter, the late Mrs. Daisy Ryman

Coggins of Atlanta, have been made available. From these rollicking episodes of love and adventure, of daring and determination, some measure of the blue-eyed master of the Cumberland can be taken.

No mere swearing, drinking, gambling steamboat captain, Ryman was a hard-driving businessman so romantic that he took thirty-five guests along on his week-long honeymoon cruise up the Ohio. A tenderhearted family man, a rich man who shared his coal with the poor when it snowed, he was fierce in anger and prodigious in energy.

He was the most influential man in the development of the shipping industry up and down the 510-mile length of the Cumberland, from its Kentucky source through its Tennessee loop to its mouth at Smithland, Kentucky, where it empties into the Ohio. His fleet of thirty-three to thirty-five steamboats funneled millions of dollars' worth of farm produce into Nashville, and shipped other millions' worth of manufactured goods out. Many of the massive brick warehouses along Nashville's waterfront were built to house loads of cotton and tobacco that rolled off his boats.

Farewell parties for young sophisticates going to Europe or for young adventurers returning to Carthage ended on the deck of steamboats tied up at Nashville's wharf—all part of Ryman's line. The "high-toned entertainment" on those boats—good food and wine, coffee in the captain's quarters, dances and cards at night, and feasting and sight-seeing by day—brought romance all along the Cumberland's crooked, green-banked length.

Captain Ryman was, in fact, such a dominant figure on the Cumberland that, it is said, he once received a letter from a poor fisherman asking Ryman's permission to fish in "your river." Ryman's childhood was spent at his father's side, fishing the Cumberland and the Tennessee, learning the mystic ways of weather and water, of sandbars and ice blocks, of seines and trotlines.

Born in South Nashville on October 12, 1841, Thomas Green Ryman was grandson of a German settler in Nashville, a locksmith named Frederick Reiman ("clean man" in German). The German immigrant, with his wife and two brothers, had come to this country in the early 1800s and had his own locksmith shop in Nashville.

Frederick (who changed his name to the English spelling, Ryman) and his wife had four sons who grew up in Nashville. One of them, John, married Sarah Green of South Carolina. The eldest of their five children was Thomas Green, founder ⌐⌐ of the Ryman Steamboat Line and the Ryman Auditorium.

Captain Tom's father, John, had wanted to operate a steamboat line, and he and his brother Charles tried for a while. But it was a hazardous and highly competitive business, and John Ryman gave it up and returned to commercial fishing. When Tom Ryman was ten years old, the family moved to Chattanooga for ten years, but after he returned to Nashville at age twenty, he had no other home the rest of his life.

He had helped his father manufacture ice commercially by filling flatboats with a few inches of water at a time and tying them up under the shade of a Chattanooga bluff where the winter sun never shone. As the ice froze, he would add more water until the ice reached the desired thickness. Then he cut it up in huge blocks and stored it underground for summer sale.

Young Tom Ryman, like Tom Sawyer, was impatient with school and eager to be on his own, but he learned stern discipline at home. One of his grandmothers, Amy Roberts Green from South Carolina, was a devout Episcopalian, and her father's family had been leaders in that faith in the Shenandoah Valley. It was that devoted grandmother who "sewed padding in Tom's pants when he was to be whipped in school."

In Nashville, Tom's parents were pillars in the Elm Street Methodist Church, and he attended services there. He grew up in a home where there were family prayers twice a day, and his sisters, in finishing school, studied the piano and learned to do fine needlework.

Tom Ryman was seventeen years old when he launched his own fishing business in 1858, operating out of Chattanooga. James S. Tyner, then an eleven-year-old Chattanooga boy who "took to water like a duck," went to work for Tom Ryman, and that was the beginning of a lifetime friendship between the two men—both eventually steamboat captains and sometime partners in business.

"That first job assigned to me by Captain Tom was digging worms (to supply fishermen)," Tyner wrote years later.

During the Civil War, Tom Ryman sold fish to Confederate troops up and down the Tennessee and Cumberland. Once when he was delivering them, he was mysteriously "arrested and imprisoned by the Yankees" in Nashville, but in a few days he was "personally pardoned by Andrew Johnson," military governor at the time.

"In gratitude for the governor's clemency, he cleaned and prepared the best fish he could find, and proceeded to the Governor's mansion to deliver it," Mrs. Coggins wrote. "The governor was very pleased and gracious."

Tom, always affable and venturesome, settled down to helping support his mother and younger brothers and sisters in Nashville after his father died in 1864. Tom had a great partner in his mother, who helped him save the three thousand dollars he needed to buy his own steamboat and leave fishing behind forever.

As a fisherman, he had watched the need for good transportation grow. Farmers in the hills of East Tennessee had no way to get their crops and cattle to market except by raft. They would bind logs together to make rafts, packing mud in the cracks to make a firm flooring. In the center of the raft they would build the mud up to a thickness to support their stove without danger of fire, and they would build a brush arbor hut around the stove to protect the crew from wind and weather.

Making the hazardous voyage by raft, threatened by protruding rocks or broken trees at shallows and sandbars, the river men might travel seven days or more from their hill homes to Nashville with their cargo of chickens, tobacco, meat, or moonshine. The back-breaking work of steering the rafts meant alertness around the clock, and by the time the men got to Nashville, they were ready to celebrate. They would sell their produce, sell their rafts to lumber yards, and take in town life for a few days.

"They had a glorious time doing the town, and as Nashville had plenty of saloons, they got plenty drunk," Mrs. Coggins wrote. "They bought a horse and rode home if they could—if they had not spent too much of their money on liquor."

Tom Ryman's ambition was to own a line of steamboats that could ship produce from Cumberland River towns to Nashville, and haul goods and passengers both ways. That included the poor raftsmen returning to their hill homes.

By 1867 Tom Ryman had saved enough to buy his own steamboat, and he made careful preparation for his own trip by raft to New Orleans to make the purchase. His mother sewed the three thousand dollars cash inside the lining of his coat and cautioned him not to remove the coat until he paid for the boat.

For that momentous trip, the twenty-six-year-old Ryman had planned everything but the weather. As the raft traveled down the Mississippi, the days grew hotter. Sleeping in a brush arbor on the mud floor, the meticulous Ryman was miserable in the steamy coat that he dared not remove. But in New Orleans, he soon found the boat he was looking for— the *Alpha*, marvelously named for the first boat in a fleet. That little boat, which had seen service in the Civil War, was "not palatial, but a good boat," Judge Byrd Douglas wrote in his invaluable book, *Steamboatin' on the Cumberland*.

Having no knowledge of the Mississippi, Ryman hired a pilot to take the cherished boat to Nashville, but he and the pilot quarreled, and Ryman, "in his usual impulsive way, fired the pilot and determined to take his boat home alone." As it turned out, the *Alpha* was not only a steady money-maker; it was the setting for one of the most picturesque wedding trips ever.

Tom Ryman met his bride-to-be, Mary Elizabeth Baugh of Franklin, after she had graduated from an Episcopal school in Franklin and was a boarding student at Franklin College, near Nashville. The latter college, run by two scholarly English brothers, Tolbert and A. J. Fanning, was rigorous in its training.

Among the students was Tom Ryman's sister, Susan, and she and Mary Elizabeth Baugh were roommates. At day-break, Susan Ryman had her practice session at the school's only piano, in the assembly hall, and Elizabeth would get up at 4 A.M. to keep her company as she practiced.

Once when Elizabeth was going home with her friend Susan Ryman for the weekend, Tom Ryman drove out to the school to pick them up. Ryman said later it was love at first sight. As he drove the horse and buggy, he noted that she was not only extremely pretty but too shy to talk to him.

Ryman, six years older than Elizabeth, courted her for over a year and was twenty-seven when he married.

The wedding, on February 3, 1869, in the parlor of the bride's home on Columbia Pike, near Franklin, was at 8 A.M.— just in time for members of the wedding party to catch the nine o'clock train for Nashville.

The bride, slender and beautiful in a dress of "blue empress cloth trimmed in white alpaca silk with a long train," was fetching with her short hair "in curls all over her head." (She had cut it when she had typhoid fever the summer before.) Her only attendants were her sister, Alabama (called "Sis Tom") and Ryman's sister, Susan. Sis Tom (later Mrs. John A. Roundtree) and Susan wore dresses of "lavender grey with train trimming in black silk ruffles, three deep pinked on the edge, or picoted as we would say now," Sis Tom wrote. The men wore "Prince Albert broadcloth." Groomsmen were steamboat captain William Gracey and William Crutcher, and the guest list included some of the best-known riverboat captains on the Cumberland.

Captain Gracey, best man at the wedding, was captain of Ryman's boat, the *Alpha*—chartered for a week by the owner to take thirty-five guests of the bride and groom on a one-week cruise from Nashville to Evansville, Indiana. After the wedding in Franklin, the wedding party had an hour's train ride before arriving in Nashville. From the station, Ryman took his bride to his mother's home for a brief visit with her and two of his young sisters. Ryman's sisters joined the other guests for the cruise on the *Alpha*, and they all drove down to the wharf to board the festive boat—her flags waving and her own dance band playing on deck.

After dinner, when the dancing began, Captain Gracey took a lot of teasing about being the only one aboard who did not know how to dance. He promised to learn, and next morning, before dawn, he was discovered alone, "behind one of the smoke stacks, shuffling his feet, trying to learn how to dance."

Gracey became so enchanted with dancing that Ryman could "hardly keep him in the ship's office long enough to attend to his business."

That morning, at Clarksville, they picked up more guests for the wedding cruise, including Matthew Gracey, already a leading figure in the packet business. When the boat reached Eddyville, Kentucky, near the point where the Cumberland empties into the Ohio, they took aboard more members of the wedding party.

On board and on land, they played games, played jokes on each other, sang, danced, and feasted. When the *Alpha* pulled into port for water and fuel and other supplies, the guests went sight-seeing. They had their pictures made in Evansville, Indiana, and got weighed at a grain elevator in Shawneetown. The bride weighed 117 pounds, Sis Tom dutifully recorded.

"We had a rare week of pleasure," Sis Tom summed up the venture. "Everything was done for our pleasure and comfort. We danced in the morning, afternoon and evening."

On the way back to Nashville, shortly after the *Alpha* left the Ohio for the homeward run on the Cumberland, the wedding party got a taste of riverboating rivalry. Captain Ryman had his boat and had his bride. Now he wanted victory in a race.

"We encountered a rival boat, the *Tyrone*, and the race was on," Sis Tom wrote. "The passengers and crew on each boat were soon aroused to the highest pitch of rivalry, the jibes and shouts passing to and fro. . . . Once the boats touched each other when one of the rousters jumped aboard the *Tyrone*, grabbed a rival rouster and dragged him aboard the *Alpha*. He soon got himself loose and made a spring and regained the *Tyrone*. . . ."

The *Tyrone* began to shoot out front, and as it sped ahead, its jubilant passengers taunted the *Alpha* crowd by waving their handkerchiefs in farewell.

"The jibes and guys were something fierce," Sis Tom wrote. "Tom Ryman could not stand it."

"He rushed below, said something to the fireman and the engineer, and the thing was done. Soon we were speeding along, gaining at each stroke. Once more the excitement became intense, but we surged ahead, and as we passed, with shouts and jeers, and the band playing, waving our handkerchiefs in farewell, one of our party wept . . . as though the parting were forever. . . . We sailed away, proud of the victory, and the *Tyrone*, seeing herself defeated, soon landed to cover her chagrin."

On the last night aboard, the wedding party decided to "get up before breakfast and have a dance forward, which we did," and "as soon as breakfast was over, the whistle blew for Nashville, and the party broke up, never again to meet as a whole."

In the years to come, when Elizabeth Ryman traveled the Cumberland with her husband, she "always shed a tear" when she passed the mouth of the Harpeth—the little river that flowed past her home town, Franklin. But she loved traveling on Tom's boats, acting as official hostess—introducing passengers to each other, seeing that each had a partner at the dances and that all had congenial company at the table.

"My father said Mother was a fine hostess and helper," one of their daughters, Mrs. Coggins, wrote. "Mother helped him to build up his business. Her great good sense and sincere interest in the passengers gave her an intelligent concept of how she could help him. She made many friends—friends of a life time."

She and Captain Tom had ten children, the first three born in Franklin and the other seven in Nashville. Three died in infancy, and the other seven grew to adulthood and survived Captain Tom. Mrs. Ryman—as practical and efficient as Tom was free-handed and daring—ran a tight ship, both at home and on the river.

They lived in two different homes in South Nashville, the second a big white frame house high on Rutledge Hill. Captain Tom selected the site on top of an old rock quarry because it offered a magnificent view of the river and was surrounded by some of the most imposing homes in the city—all close to the old University of Nashville, cultural center of that era. They had moved in by 1885.

Captain Tom could sit at his table and look over the treetops of his lawn, down to the bottom of the hill where his boats churned the Cumberland with their paddlewheels. He could walk through his own garden and see which of his boats was arriving or departing Nashville on time.

If he had a boat leaving for the Ohio, he never "rested easy" until a telephone call from Clarksville notified him that the boat had passed the drawbridge safely. He never forgot the day one of his boats was approaching the Clarksville bridge and blew the whistle to signal the drawbridge to open. The bridge opened, but a train crew failed to get the signal, and the engine, mail car, and baggage car ran off the bridge and into the river. Miraculously, all but two of the crew escaped.

The river, one way or another, was center of the Ryman household. Telephone calls in the middle of the night might mean fire or explosion or sinking of a boat, or disaster on the pontoon bridge Tom built.

Part of the charm of the Ryman home with its two little towers and seven gables was the view of the suspension bridge linking downtown Nashville with East Nashville. When that bridge weakened and had to be dismantled, the project made radical changes in the Ryman household's routine. For Captain Ryman got the contract for building and operating the pontoon bridge that handled the traffic while a new bridge was being built, and he was up before dawn every day driving through the ornate gates to see that all went well.

"This bridge was simply a series of small boats, side by side across the river, with a strong floor of heavy planks connecting them," Mrs. Coggins wrote. "When all this building was going on and the old bridge was being destroyed, all at the same time, the scene was one of tremendous activity, noise and labor. Many Negroes were employed, and they often sang as they worked. . . . It all looked dangerous, as indeed it was. . . . This time was strenuous for all of us because we had breakfast very early so that my father could be on the scene when work began. He was prompt, always ahead of time. All the rivermen in his employ were kept busy. He wanted all to be on hand when he arrived."

One of the clerks in Ryman's office—headquarters for the Ryman Line—slept over the office. Mrs. Coggins wrote, "He said the sound of Papa's horse rattling down Market Street so early in the morning was his signal to rise quickly. He would just have time to dress, seize a canoe at the wharf and be at the scene of action by the time Papa could drive across the bridge."

There was something about the firm-mouthed, quiet Captain Ryman that "carried to all who knew him the impression of his great reserve power." He never let his workers down, and they tried hard to measure up to his expectations.

The hazards of keeping the bridge open were constant, and if the swift current swept one of the supporting boats loose, all traffic had to halt until repairs were completed. "If this happened at night, our telephone would ring urgently and we would hear Papa hurrying out the door to see about the trouble," Mrs. Coggins wrote.

To pay for all of that service, the pontoon bridge charged a small fee from all carriages. The clerk who collected the toll, from a small office at one end of the bridge, had difficulty with some travelers.

"The great ladies in fine carriages gave the most trouble," Mrs. Coggins said. "One of these ladies, very handsome, imposing, in a fine carriage with a liveried driver, stopped and became very angry when the clerk came out to collect the toll. 'This is an intolerable outrage!' the lady protested. 'I absolutely refuse to pay for it. Drive on, James!'"

This story of the ludicrous lady became a favorite of the Ryman family.

Ryman's home, with its two frame towers caught in a cluster of brick and stone towers in genteel old South Nashville, was a treasured haven to the riverboat captain. He selected the many magnolia trees for the half-acre lot stretching toward the river, and bordered it with elm trees that were large when he planted them. That in itself was no small feat, for Ryman had to blast out ten-foot holes in the rocky hill to plant each tree. And Ryman so loved his trees and garden that he had a gardener water them regularly all summer and brush the snow off the leaves in winter to keep them from breaking.

Across the street from the Ryman home was the old Howard School with its tall bell tower. The Ryman children measured their days by its tolling. "That great bell in the lofty tower had rung at 8 o'clock for many years, and the Ryman house needed no other signal to be ready for school," Mrs. Coggins wrote. "There was still a few more minutes before tardy could be charged against a child."

The Ryman children were awakened with a "rising bell"

half an hour before breakfast every morning. "We had to be completely dressed, ready for school, because immediately after breakfast, Mrs. Ryman had family prayers in the living room," Tom Ryman's daughter recalled the well-regulated household.

"Every child had to learn the Sunday School lesson for the next Sunday—every day learning a little more. By Saturday, we were expected to really know it. . . . On week days, the great bell would end the family prayer meeting, when everybody went to school."

Tom Ryman, the riverboat captain who funneled a river's riches into Nashville and left an auditorium behind as a monument to his religion, wanted to be sure his children shared in it.

When Captain Tom "Got Religion"

Back in Capt. Tom Ryman's day—the heyday of steamboat traffic on the Cumberland—his fleet of boats hauled more passengers and freight than any other line. And "steamboatin' wasn't exactly a lemonade Lucy's life."

Social life on the boats as well as in town revolved around the bar, and getting the bar concession on one of the Ryman boats meant a good income. Captain Ryman, as owner of some thirty-four boats, got a percentage of the profits.

So when the word went out that Captain Tom had "got religion" at Sam Jones's big tent meeting in 1885, one of the many myths about him sprang up. "They say he went down to his boat the next day and dumped every bottle of whiskey overboard and never drank any of the stuff again," the popular story went.

Actually Ryman had many boats at the time, and it would have been impossible to reach all of them, scattered up and down the Cumberland and Ohio, to empty bottles in one day. Moreover, the liquor belonged to the men who owned the bar concessions, not to Ryman.

"What he did was to wait until the contract ran out on the bar concession on each boat," his granddaughter, Mrs. Elizabeth Coggins Jones of Atlanta, owner of the valuable memoirs written by Ryman's daughter, explained in a recent interview. Mrs. Jones inherited the memoirs from her mother, Mrs. Daisy Ryman Coggins.

There were some eighty-one steamboats plying the Cumberland then, all of them competing for passengers and freight. So closing the bars on all of his boats meant a sizable loss to Captain Ryman. He lost not only his percentage of profits from the bars, but also the customers who preferred traveling on a boat that had a bar.

But Ryman never turned back, once he had mapped his course. He had been operating Ryman Line, Inc., with headquarters near the river, for eighteen years, when Sam Jones held his tent meeting in 1885. No other businessman in Nashville had a higher reputation for honesty and fair dealing. No other man on the Cumberland had a more devoted following. When emergencies struck, when other men despaired of rescuing a boat from sandbar or ice, fire or boiler explosion, they counted on Captain Tom to find a way. From the time he bought his first steamboat, the *Alpha*, in New Orleans in 1867 and took it partway to Nashville himself—in spite of the fact that he was unfamiliar with the treacherous Mississippi—legends began to grow around him.

Competing with 296 packets on the Cumberland in the 1860s, Ryman made so much money off his well-run *Alpha*— a sound little boat with no fancy trimmings but plenty of dependable service—that he could afford a new boat built to his specifications four years later. Ryman took his wife and baby daughter, Daisy, with him to Evansville, Indiana, to live while he supervised.

"Mamma and Daisy saw the *Eddyville* launched at Evansville," a younger sister, Mrs. Leslie Ryman Barton, wrote in 1919. "The *Eddyville* was begun on Friday, launched on Friday and began her first trip on a Friday in January, 1872."

Ryman named the *Eddyville* in honor of the Kentucky town on the Cumberland near the point where it empties into the Ohio. He had many friends there, some of whom had gone on the wedding cruise up the Ohio with him and his bride two years before. And when the *Eddyville* put in at that friendly town, "the ladies of Eddyville presented the boat with a handsome silver service." Long after Captain Tom and the *Eddyville* were gone, his children cherished that token of friendship.

"The tray has an inscription, and what is left of this water service is still in the family," Ryman's daughter, Mrs. Coggins, wrote in 1952. "The *Eddyville* was a very pretty boat with a very pretty cabin."

The cabins, or parlors, of the steamboats had pianos for paid band members to play, but often passengers entertained at the piano. Ryman's own daughters, when they were children, loved nothing so much as a cruise up and down the rivers—the pets of captains who invited them to four o'clock coffee in the pilot house if they were good.

Captain of the *Eddyville* was Ryman's old friend James Tyner, whom he had first employed when they were both boys in the commercial fishing business near Chattanooga. Captain Tyner, sometime part-owner of Ryman's boats, revered Ryman as the "dominant figure on the Cumberland."

"There was never a man so well acquainted with the Cumberland as he was," Tyner wrote. "When the scepter fell from his hands, there was no one to replace him."

Whether it was dealing with shippers whose grain he took

to Nashville from the Midwest, or warehouse owners or ship-builders or deckhands or rowdy roustabouts who loaded and unloaded his many boats, Ryman moved quietly, firmly, decisively.

Ryman himself said he was no betting man, except for twelve thousand dollars he won on Grover Cleveland's election in 1884, but river men used to put up bets on Ryman's ingenuity. In February, 1872, when five packets were locked in the frozen Ohio near Carrsville, Kentucky, word came that one of the doomed boats was Ryman's.

"Papa's boat was in the lot," Mrs. Barton wrote. "Bets were made in Nashville that if a boat was saved, it would be Tom Ryman's boat. Papa placed jugs under the ice, equipped with powder and fuse, blew up the ice, and Papa went to bat with his boat!"

Shifting sands and swift currents created sandbars where there had been none before. Floodwaters swept dead trees off the river banks, and sometimes their brittle limbs hidden under the water's surface ripped lethal holes in the bottom of boats.

One night Ryman's boat, "running another trip up river, ran a tree up into her hull through the deck," Mrs. Barton wrote. How to unsnag the heavy boat from the daggerlike limb? "He sawed off the tree limb from inside the hull, even with the bottom of the boat, and then he looked for something tough and slick enough to help ease the boat off the sawed limb. He took a ham skin, put it on the tree from the inside of the hull and backed the boat off!"

The Cumberland traffic had its share of fire and boiler explosions, and Ryman searched for the strongest materials to protect his boats. "Papa always secured iron for boilers from Hillman Iron Works, which guaranteed them never to blow up, and filled the guarantee," Mrs. Barton wrote.

Ryman's boats, among the finest on the Cumberland, included two named for a Nashville father and son, B. S. and I. T. Rhea, two leading businessmen—owners of terminals for storing grain and of a steamboat line on the Tennessee. The Rheas, both friends of Ryman's, cooperated with him in the battle of the 1880s to keep railroads in a subsidiary role in the shipping business. The Rheas, as well as Ryman, cut their shipping rates and offered free storage in Nashville for grain shipped in from the Midwest by boat and shipped out of Nashville by rail to customers who lived far from the river.

Tons of produce flowed into Nashville in the 1890s, and lumber was a growing load. Because of the leadership of fighting Tom Ryman, riverboats were still giving stiff competiton to trains as late as 1895. In that year, thirty thousand passengers rode the Nashville packets. Ryman never charged a church for shipping building material, whether lumber, bricks, or stone, and he never charged fare for salesmen whose companies shipped their goods on his packets.

There were trade advantages to shippers who divided their shipping between boat and train, shipping as far as they could by boat and then shifting to train. Ryman named boats for Nashville businessmen whose companies shipped their goods by his boats. He had boats named the *H. W. Buttorff*, the *Sam J. Keith*, and the *Bob Dudley*. The *J. P. Drouillard*, the *Alex Perry*, the *Reuben Dunbar*, the *W. K. Cherry*, and the *James K. White* rode the Cumberland proudly.

But trains were faster, and their tracks threaded the countryside to towns no boat had ever seen. Ryman, for all his clever negotiating with railroads and terminals and shippers, was fighting for his steamboats' life by the end of the century, when an accident on a viaduct—a collision between his buggy and a truck—brought on his final illness three years later.

But he still dreamed of the glorious days when boats like

the *B. S. Rhea*, one of the finest in his fleet, would capture the trade again. "The *B. S. Rhea* was beautifully equipped and one of the best managed packets on the Cumberland," the late Byrd Douglas wrote in his book, *Steamboatin' on the Cumberland.*

The boat named for Rhea's son, I. T. Rhea, was a "splendid boat and one of the most popular," Douglas wrote. But it was a hard-luck boat. "The *I. T. Rhea* sank 13 times and always on the 13th of the month," Mrs. Coggins wrote. "The last time, in 1895, she sank in the Upper Cumberland, and Captain Ryman refused to raise her—let her machinery lay and rust in the water."

But Mrs. Coggins remembered the lucky boats, the ones she and her brothers and sisters traveled on in the 1880s and 1890s. When Ryman, a slender, hard-muscled man "of fine physique," took them aboard, the wonder of river life captivated them.

"The scenery down the Cumberland and up the Ohio was varied and beautiful," Mrs. Coggins wrote. "The shores touched Kentucky and Indiana. The great width of the river often looked like a lake and it was very beautiful—especially at sunset when favored passengers gathered in the pilot house. When the Ryman children were aboard, they made it convenient to be in the pilot house at 4 o'clock, because coffee is always served at that hour, and if the pilot was good-natured, he could speak to the steward through one of the three speaking tubes handy and order coffee for the visitors. He would also let a favorite child blow the whistle for the landing."

When things got tense in the pilot house, the children knew by the look in the captain's eyes to tiptoe out. There were, after all, endless other attractions. "Sometimes there were interesting people in the ladies' cabin—and if there was no amusement inside, there was something exciting outside,"

Mrs. Coggins wrote. "If a lot of cattle were being brought aboard, it was as great as a circus to see the deck hands persuade reluctant cows to come aboard. Sometimes the cows resisted mightily and dragged these colored men back to the shore and wound the long ropes by which they were led around a convenient tree. They were very clever at giving all the trouble they could, but once aboard, on the lower deck, safely installed and well fed, the cows were quiet and contented."

The Ryman children were overawed by the strength of deckhands and roustabouts who tugged at balking cattle and unloaded huge hogsheads of tobacco. Their vocabulary was colorful, and the songs they sang as the boats backed off from the wharf were richly melodious.

Sometimes, in spite of skill and muscle, hogsheads of tobacco would slip off the loading ramp into the river, and only "the hardest work and ingenuity" could rescue them.

"These heavy things were stored on the lower deck, of course, while lighter weight things were sometimes crowded along the guard rails," Mrs. Coggins wrote. "Some times they were loaded beside the pretty white balustrade at the edge of the passenger deck. If these spaces were occupied by bags of peanuts, for instance, it was a strong temptation to make a hole in the tow sack and steal a handful."

Mrs. Coggins said she had seen light buggies loaded on the hurricane deck, "this being the name of the roof of the passenger deck."

"Here was the Texas—sleeping quarters for the crew—atop the pilot house," she explained. "It was a fascinating life—the rhythmic throb of the engines was pleasant to hear, the great wheel at the back was pleasant to watch as it threw the water up and over the wheel, making a rainbow if the sun was shining."

Home on the high hill in South Nashville, overlooking the river, was just as pleasant for Captain Ryman and his family. Accustomed to fine food, bought in quantities for his fleet of boats and their dining rooms, he kept his own cellar at the big white house stored with goodies. "There was always a box of oranges in the house, and always a barrel of apples," Mrs. Coggins wrote. "He bought everything wholesale. We had large storerooms—a barrel of sugar, 50 pounds of lard, etc. In my childhood, there was a flour factory in the next block, and Papa bought flour from his friend Noel there, in wooden barrels."

Just because Ryman "liked ambrosia very much," he had a "barrel of coconuts sent to Mother one day to make ambrosia."

"It was a very good thing that my mother was a woman of great practical sense," Daisy Coggins wrote. "She was the balance wheel that his disposition needed." One morning as snow fell thicker by the moment, Mose, the yardman at the Ryman home, was out early shaking the snow off the magnolia trees. Captain Ryman called him in.

"Mose, there's lots of suffering on Rolling Mill Hill this morning," Ryman said. "Many people haven't fire. Go over there and tell anybody who hasn't coal to come to my cellar with a tow sack. They can take a sack full home."

The response was quick. The cellar was full of coal that Ryman had bought at low cost the summer before and shipped on his own boats from Kentucky mines. Feeling that the supply was practically inexhaustible, he enjoyed sharing it.

When he came home for midday dinner, he voted down his wife's suggestion that they shut the cellar door. He wanted no one to be without fire. But by dark the cellar was empty. Luckily, Mrs. Ryman had filled all the "coal vases" in the house to supply their many grates. And first thing next morning Ryman had to order coal at retail prices.

Captain Ryman, in 1885, was forty-three years old and father of eight children, at the height of his business career, when he dropped in one night to hear Rev. Sam Jones, famous revivalist, preach in a tent. Ryman was never the same again. The evangelist preached soul-shaking sermons on the evils of drink, and Captain Ryman, well aware of the problems all up and down the river, repented of operating bars that would tempt others.

His new religious fervor so gripped Ryman that he wanted all others to share it. As he came out of the tent and found part of the crowd outside, he determined to build a tremendous tabernacle where Nashvillians of all faiths could worship together any season of the year. Ryman took his idea to Jones, and his enthusiasm was contagious. But the YMCA was in the midst of a fund-raising campaign for a new building, and Ryman decided to put off his drive until the YMCA had reached its goal.

Meanwhile, he had other ways of sharing his religion with others. He established a mission for steamboat men next door to his office, near the river. He employed a full-time minister to hold nightly services there, and hired a teacher for night school for steamboat men and their families. His generosity to Nashville's poor reached in all directions. Ryman built a "Gospel Wagon" to take the gospel to neighborhoods without churches, and on Sunday afternoons, in the business district, streetcars and other traffic stopped while the Gospel Wagon—complete with pulpit, organ, and choir—held forth.

At the same time, he was soliciting donations for the tabernacle. When Sam Jones returned to Nashville in 1889 for another revival, a total of twenty-two thousand dollars was raised for the tabernacle at the final service. That same year, Ryman got a charter for the tabernacle and bought a lot (where the auditorium still stands) for ten thousand dollars. That summer the foundation of massive stone was laid. By the spring of 1890, the brick walls of Union Gospel Tabernacle were built to a height of about six feet.

A canvas roof was stretched over the walls so that Nashville could welcome Jones back for another revival series on Sunday, March 25, 1890. Jones packed the crowds in—ten thousand a day—and raised $13,500 more toward the building fund.

Nashvillians, rich and poor, reached deep in their pockets to pay for the great bleak barn of a building with its marvelous acoustics and its earnest pews. By 1892 the tabernacle (called Union because it was to unify all faiths) was near enough to completion to house another revival by Jones. But the building had been planned for a variety of events that would contribute to the "religion, morality, and elevation of humanity to a higher plane and more usefulness," and it was already fulfilling the wider purpose.

World-famous lecturers and musicians were filling the auditorium, and in revivals in 1894 and 1895 Jones was still appealing to the city to help pay for the building and its pews. The big goal in 1897 was to add a gallery around three sides, to hold the Confederate Veterans' reunion—the biggest convention thus far. The veterans themselves contributed a substantial amount, and that fact is commemorated in the name, Confederate Gallery, painted on the balcony railing. With that added space, the tabernacle could hold four thousand.

In 1900 Sam Jones announced that the building had already cost a hundred thousand dollars, and Ryman had borne the major burden of the debt and the interest on it. Nobody could estimate how many miles Ryman walked in trying to raise money for the tabernacle, Jones said. Ryman welcomed the Chautauqua and Lyceum lectures and concerts that helped pay the bills, but he protested the use of the tabernacle for "politics" and demanded that it be used by those who "respect God's love and the building."

He was pleased when William Jennings Bryan, Frances E. Willard (president of the Women's Christian Temperance Union), and Mrs. Carry Nation (hatchet-wielding dry) spoke there. At the same time, concerts by artists like Caruso and John McCormack, Paderewski and Galli-Curci, Pavlova and Nijinsky, were making the auditorium a celebrated spot. In spite of inadequacies in comfort, both for audience and for performers backstage, the auditorium became a unique experience. Actresses like Sarah Bernhardt and Katharine Cornell cherished it for the acoustics that took whispers to the last row.

For at least five years before Ryman's death, Nashville business leaders—well aware of the work and fortune he had poured into the building—had proposed changing the name to Ryman Auditorium. Each time, Ryman, president of the board, voted the idea down. But when he died on December 23, 1904, after a long and painful illness, there was no one left to oppose it.

Ryman was sixty-three years old when he died. For days before his death, newspapers over the state carried front-page bulletins on his worsening condition. At the funeral on Christmas Day, 1904, Nashville forgot its holiday joy and packed the tabernacle to honor the man who had given the city its vast auditorium.

For an hour and a half before the 2:30 P.M. service, crowds began filing past the doors draped in flags and funereal black and white. The balcony rail was draped in black and white from one end to the other, while flags hung below and bunting was wound around each post.

The somber stage, with mountains of flowers and a hundred leading businessmen and steamboat captains seated there, was centered with the cherry coffin. The great Sam Jones himself preached the funeral sermon. A close friend of Ryman's, Jones had often been a guest in the Ryman home, and he said he would keep the services short, in keeping with the wishes of the "gentle man of child-like faith."

"A purer, stronger, nobler man, truer to God than he, I have never met," Jones said.

There were tributes from near and far to the "Father of the Tabernacle," and Jones wound up the poignant services by asking for a vote on his proposal that the tabernacle be named Ryman Auditorium. As one, the audience of four thousand rose to signify their agreement, and editorials for days to come cited organizations that had voted agreement. When the Grand Ole Opry took over the auditorium and changed its name, forgetting the brave riverboat captain who had built it, there were still many who never considered calling it anything but The Ryman.

The structure, now officially listed as a building of historic and architectural significance, "has one of the most star-studded histories of the performing arts in the United States," famed architecture critic Ada Louise Huxtable wrote in the *New York Times* on May 13, 1973. Destruction of the historic landmark was for a time threatened, with the owners, the National Life and Accident Insurance Company, considering taking apart the bricks of the "real thing" to provide an imitation chapel at Opryland, Miss Huxtable said.

That would have angered Captain Ryman. If there was anything he was, it was the "real thing."

George Washington Sent Augustin Gattinger

It was a George Washington's birthday party Augustin Gattinger would remember the rest of his life. Never before had Germany held such a celebration, and never again would Gattinger feel the thrill of freedom so poignantly. And because young Gattinger, then a medical student at the University of Munich, dared celebrate Washington's birthday so boldly that February 22, 1849, Nashville and Tennessee benefit today.

But blue-eyed, twenty-four-year-old Gattinger had no thought of Tennessee that chilly February day in Germany, as he and hundreds of other students and faculty members boiled in rage at the freedoms denied them by the German government. Only a few days before, some two hundred citizens of the poetic city of Munich had met secretly to determine the best method of getting out of their country and fleeing to America. They were people of ample means— "Discontented citizens, artists, professional men, mechanics and farmers, people of good standing in society." All they wanted was freedom.

That gave Gattinger and some of his fellow students an idea. Since they could not demonstrate openly, they could at least throw a party in honor of Washington, the freedom fighter. The "solemn fete" they planned was a "proceeding never heard of before," Gattinger said, but it was "fully in accord with the sentiments of this party, which in these turbulent times represented the liberal movement in the University."

The highly secret party was held late at night, in the university area. High point of the proceedings was the reading of Washington's farewell address. Loud shouts of approval punctuated that speech and excerpts from speeches by Thomas Jefferson, Benjamin Franklin, and "other heroes." Their eulogies brought "fervent and unreserved" response.

Gattinger, in his last term as a medical student, left the room in a glow of patriotic fervor. He and the other students congratulated themselves that they had heard freedom ring.

It rang loudly enough to reach university and city authorities almost immediately. Quickly Gattinger and other leaders were called before the officials. All students involved were dismissed from the university. Gattinger, an earnest young man whose hobby was walking the woods in pursuit of new plants for his botany collection, would not be allowed to get his medical degree. Moreover, city authorities told him he would have to go to prison or leave the country.

Stunned at the sudden turn in his quiet life, in a city where his father had been a top official and his home had been a haven of comfort and learning, Gattinger rushed to his sweetheart, Josephine Dury, with the tragic news. Would she marry him and go to America with him? Josephine said yes. Then she turned to her thirty-two-year-old brother, George Dury, and asked him if he would come to America. A portrait painter already established in Munich, he was courting a nineteen-year-old girl, Catherine Sheafer.

Would Catherine marry George Dury, so that the four of them could go to America together? Catherine said yes, and within a month she was writing in her diary: "Today, Monday, the 25th of March, 1849, I said good-bye to beautiful, friendly St. Martin—place of my birth and my childhood, to my beloved, dear good parents, brothers, sisters, and friends. Good-bye may be forever, because my good George has chosen for me a new home on another continent."

The two couples left Munich at dawn on April 15, and journeyed to Le Havre, on the southern coast of France, to sail on a three-masted ship appropriately named *Bavaria*. On the morning of their sailing, April 24, 1849, the two couples met at the American consulate at Le Havre to be married. That afternoon, with ten other young couples from Bavaria, they set sail for a new life across the Atlantic.

Gattinger never pretended that leaving his beautiful mountain land of Bavaria was easy. "The severance from beloved friends and the ancestral soil is a bitter and mournful task," he wrote fifty-two years later. "But the genius of love mitigated my distress, for the one whom I had chosen for my companion through the turmoil of life consented to go with me."

The voyage to America took thirty-two days, and as they sighted the shore line at New York, the Durys and the Gattingers were standing at the rail with tears streaming down their faces.

"Oh, what an indescribable feeling," Catherine Dury wrote. "Tears of joy ran out almost everybody's eyes. . . . New York! What a grand sight! This sea of buildings, these ships, the bustle, these beautiful magnificent mansions along the entire coast! . . . 'Let us make our tabernacle here.' This prayer sprang out of my heart."

But the Durys and the Gattingers did not tarry in New York, for they knew of the Swiss-German settlement called Wartburg in Morgan County, Tennessee. They took a train to the end of the line, in Dalton, Georgia, and a stagecoach from there to Chattanooga, where they arrived early in July, 1849.

Gattinger was entranced with the dramatic scenery at Chattanooga, because it made him think of the hills of Bavaria. So they took a side-wheeled steamer up the Clinch River and landed at Kingston, to be "base of operations for exploring the vicinity."

"Weary of traveling and wishing to enter the practice of my profession, I was easily fascinated by a romantic spot called Cave Springs, eight miles to the west of Kingston," Gattinger wrote. He bought out the practice of an older doctor just leaving to go West, and he and his brother-in-law, Dury, bought farm land there. But neither knew anything about farming, and Dury soon moved with his bride to Nashville to paint portraits of the state's leaders and teach art at the Nashville Female Academy.

The Durys were living in Nashville on June 5, 1850, when their first child, Augusta Katharina Carolina, was born. She was the first of three children. The third, George Carl, later founded Dury's store, specializing in art and photographic supplies, on Union Street.

Meantime, for almost fifteen years, Dr. Gattinger rode his horse over hundreds of backwoods miles in East Tennessee, calling on patients and pursuing his great hobby—the study of plants. Ice on his boots froze him to the stirrups on some of his calls to distant patients and his body grew stooped with rheumatism. Yet when the weather was sunny, the plants and rocks to be studied on the mountain slopes enthralled him. In the silent woods of East Tennessee, a whole new world of plants—as clear to him in their relationship as cousins and uncles and aunts—was waiting to be studied and cataloged.

"The transfer from a buoyant German city to this silent retreat was to me a stimulus to concentrate my attention outside of my professional duties and equestrian hardships to the study of botany and geology of the country," Dr. Gattinger recalled those lonely days.

He and Mrs. Gattinger had three daughters—Augusta, Wilhelmina, and Penelope (known to friends as Gussie, Minnie, and Pennie)—and he practiced medicine first at Cave Springs, then in Charleston (Bradley County) and Ducktown, where he was resident physician at the copper mines.

It was in the latter position, where he could ride the high ridges along the North Carolina and Georgia borders, that he found a botanist's and geologist's paradise. The face of the Cumberland Mountains and the Smokies became as familiar as the palm of his hand. He slept outdoors, and stood alone on the great balds of the Smokies to marvel at the wealth of wildflowers and trees, marbles and granites, below him. He collected samples, mounted them meticulously, and began a nationwide correspondence with the country's leading botanists to exchange information.

It was the beginning of one of the great herbariums of the nation, the second largest in the South. This collection of dried plants, each carefully mounted and identified, became a rich resource for scientists over the nation, and was eventually given to the University of Tennessee in Knoxville.

It was the Civil War that brought him down out of the mountains of East Tennessee and into Nashville in 1864. He had a horror of seeing this nation divided, to suffer as his native Germany had under competing governments. His pro-Union sympathies were so unpopular with his neighbors that Gattinger fled to Cleveland, Tennessee, for protection.

"In a cold, stormy March night, afoot, no money, with a small satchel for a traveling outfit, I made my way through the Ocoee gorge and reached the town of Cleveland, 40 miles distant, without an accident," he wrote. There he met Union officers who escorted him to Nashville, and after rigid examination he was commissioned as assistant surgeon in the United States Army.

Soon he sent for his wife and three young daughters, and his brother-in-law, Dury, found quarters for them in the home of a Hungarian friend, Prof. Alexander Kocsis. Mrs. Kocsis, daughter of one of Nashville's prominent families, the Overtons, turned part of her big brick home in South Nashville over to the Gattingers and they became great friends.

After the war, Professor Kocsis and his wife bought a farm near Tullahoma, and Dr. Gattinger, on visits there, made frequent "rambles" for rare plants. Tullahoma, in fact, is now immortalized in botany—as are Lavergne and Smyrna and numerous other Tennessee towns—by the plants he discovered in that area (*Arguta tullahoma*, for instance).

When he visited Tullahoma, Dr. Gattinger would strike out across the fields with a bright young black boy who worked for Professor Kocsis and seemed eager to learn more about plants. But one day, after an hour in the field, the boy came running back to the Kocsis house in a state of terror. "That doctor's gone stark raving crazy in the woods!" he sounded the alarm. "I ran away before he could catch me."

When Kocsis and his son hurried to the woods, they found the little doctor dancing with joy. He had discovered a rare jewel of a plant. "Dr. Gattinger was in a transport of exultation, jumping up and down around a tiny plant which he caressed with loving hands," Kocsis reported. "He had discovered a specimen which he had vainly sought for many years."

Gattinger, who was a curiosity to Nashvillians as he traveled about in his "peculiar" horse-drawn carriage, usually had trowel and other botanical equipment along, even as he called on patients. Meeting familiar plants was, for him, like meeting old friends. "Every tree, grass and flower had its

kindly greeting, often provoking a tender, loving caress," one
of Gattinger's friends observed.

Out of his hobby of botany, Dr. Gattinger published six
small books, some of them rare contributions to the nation's
knowledge. His herbarium eventually contained more than
four thousand species of plants found in Tennessee.

He served at various times as state botanist, and held numerous special appointments from the department of agriculture, usually to prepare books or exhibits of Tennessee's
plants and marbles for expositions over the country. One of
the surprising tasks of his career came in the five years from
1864 to 1869, when he served as state librarian, by appointment of Gov. Andrew Johnson. The little German incurred
criticism for stocking the library with books on botany,
geology, and philosophy, many of them written in German,
but Gattinger argued that Tennesseans needed to know more
about their rich resources and needed the scholarly tools to
appraise them. One great advantage of being state librarian
was that Dr. Gattinger held a railroad pass that entitled him
to travel over the state without paying, and he used that
privilege to collect plants and minerals in all directions.

It was at this time that he bought a lot in South Nashville, in the heart of the city's university community. Scientists and doctors at the University of Nashville were his close
friends, and their charming brick homes ringing the campus
were the setting for challenging conversation about everything from medicine to marble. So he selected a large corner
lot across the street from the old Carroll Street Methodist
Church. There he stood on the hillside as workmen blasted
out the rocky slope to make way for his cellar in 1869.

Then a marvelous thing happened to the little doctor.
Out of the blast fell at his feet a beautiful fossil, an ancient
shell formation so rare that nothing like it has been seen

before or since. A shell belonging to the subdivision Pteropoda, it measured more than ten inches. With rare appropriateness, botanists named the fossil for him—*Conularia gattingeri*—and museums across the country, including the Smithsonian in Washington, requested casts for their collections.

The home Dr. Gattinger built was a three-story brick, with a sunny study, a greenhouse, and a flourishing garden. There he would cultivate wild plants that captivated him, and there he would introduce other scientists to those cherished "friends."

He lived, breathed, felt passionately about ecology a century before it became a household word. He thrilled to the interplay between Tennessee's rocky hills and sandy flatlands, its marble and its wildflowers and grasses. He worried because its legislators turned the other way when he talked to them of the wealth of resources waiting to be uncovered.

There were no foundations then to finance his research, and the state paid him nothing for the work he published from time to time on Tennessee flora. The state paid only the cost of printing some of the books, and Gattinger, out of his own small earnings as a doctor, paid for the others.

He himself pursued the study "from the love and admiration of nature and the amazement about prodigy in color and form," he said. He was intrigued by the "difference between plant individuals, the changes to which they are subject, the laws which govern their growth and the part they play in the general economy of the world." He was convinced that in those studies lay the answer to all sorts of questions about mankind and the world of which he is a part.

On a typical day—April 21, 1880, for instance—he was up early to take the train from Nashville to Lavergne and explore the woods until he caught the 4 P.M. train home. The day was popping with surprises, and suddenly it was time to run for the train. Gattinger and his assistant, laden with plants all carefully annotated, were a quarter of a mile from the railway station at Lavergne when he heard the train whistle at Smyrna, seven miles away. In what must have been a comic race, the elfish little scholar and his helper, perspiring and breathless, "arrived in one dash with the train."

At the height of his career, the triumphant fifty-five-year-old Gattinger rushed home to mount his specimens from Lavergne that night. He had them in the mail the next day, on their way to Dr. Asa Gray at Cambridge, Massachusetts.

He found a rare plant in the swampy lands of West Tennessee and in the "orange sand formations near Hollow Rock, in Carroll County," and wrote a learned paper on it. He climbed the Smokies part of the way in mule-drawn wagon and the rest of the way on foot. He encountered bears and deer. He made discoveries of rare ferns and orchids on Big Frog Mountain, and almost wept at their beauty. He was one of the first to work toward the day when the Smokies would be a national park, set aside for the enjoyment of nature.

And when Tennessee celebrated its hundredth birthday in 1897 and thousands flocked to the exhibits at what is now Centennial Park, Gattinger took courage. This, he said, proved that Tennesseans would respond to beauty. He, along with Maj. E. C. Lewis, chief promoter of the centennial celebration, worked hard to see the grounds set aside as the first park for the city—the beginning of a citywide park system.

"Inspired as I was by the success of our Centennial, I felt urged to speak to the public about the necessity of making permanent and to enlarge upon such great boon," he stated to the governor in requesting state funds to publish his

Treatise on Parks and Gardens: Their Ethical Influence on Public Life and Their Sanitary Effect.

At the centennial, he said, he felt for the first time the heart of Tennessee people: "It was indeed the first time to feel in mingling with the crowds of visitors that I was living with a great and amiable people that lacked but the opportunities to show the noble qualities of a freedom-loving citizenship."

Freedom-loving. That took him back to that Washington's birthday in Munich—the Munich where, as a lonely seven-year-old boy, he plucked violets in a beautiful park as he mourned his father. He wanted Nashville to have parks like that, to enjoy the flowers. He wanted Tennessee youth to learn about the state's plants, but when he saw his vast collection of dried plants leave his South Nashville home for the University of Tennessee, the little doctor wiped the tears away.

When he gave his library of rare books on botany and geology to the University of the South at Sewanee, he liked to think of young botanists of the future poring over them. "While the pursuit of botany never brought me any financial advantages," he said, "I acknowledge that it was a mighty protection in keeping me out of the way of social corruption, and it gave me many hours of the purest enjoyment of life, and brought me in relation with many excellent men and women."

Even after he had given away his collection, he would keep collecting. "I will remain the rest of my days . . . a botanical grasshopper," he wrote in 1888. "I shall ramble about next spring, collecting as usual."

In July, 1903, when he was seventy-eight years old and still working hard to get a park system started in the state, he died of pneumonia. Friends said he had talked more and more of philosophy—of the relationship of man to his environment, of mankind's social progress. That, he said, was what led him to celebrate Washington's birthday so exuberantly on February 22, 1849.

Yellow Terror

Memphis was a soundless battlefield where victims fell silently in the hot streets and few were left to bury them. It was the stifling autumn of 1878, and the horror-stricken survivors of the worst yellow fever epidemic in the nation's history ventured outside their doors only long enough to get the supplies rationed them.

Stores were closed. Business offices, railway stations, river docks, warehouses, and churches were closed. Only the supply depot and the cemeteries were busy. "For nearly 60 days Memphis was nothing more than a vast hospital," one physician described the grisly scene.

Policemen and firemen were dead. Courts adjourned. There were few to earn wages, and few to pay them. Banks were closed most of the time. Drugstores were closed, and the druggists dead. The living walked like ghosts in the city of death. Startled by the sound of their own footsteps on the deserted streets in the middle of the day, they walked like strangers in their own city.

Newspaper reporters, editors, and printers died in such numbers that the city's leading paper dwindled to a two-page publication and the editor got it out single-handedly. Of the staff of seventy-three, only two escaped the fever, while nineteen died. The whole front page was devoted to lists of the city's dead and dying. The ads featured coffins and "cures" for yellow fever. Editorials shifted from courage to despair.

154

There was no room for obituaries.

Doctors and nurses were the gods and goddesses of the day. But they, too, fell on duty, and other doctors and nurses from over the nation came in to take their places.

Dr. Thomas O. Summers, Jr., then on the Vanderbilt medical school faculty, was the first Nashville doctor to volunteer to go to Memphis. He headed a delegation of doctors who surveyed health conditions in West Tennessee towns caught in the epidemic, and he worked among the Memphis victims until its end.

Three of his former students—all young Nashville doctors—joined him on the dangerous mission, and all three died. One of them, Dr. O. D. Bartholomew, went back on duty after having apparently recovered, but then suffered a relapse and was dead in twenty-four hours, on October 8, 1878.

"Nashville never sent a braver spirit into battle," Memphis papers wrote when Dr. Bartholomew died. "Memphis never had a better friend." The Tennessee State Library has a portrait of the blond, blue-eyed young doctor who died in the hopeless struggle. The portrait was presented to the state legislature in 1879 to commemorate his heroism, but it is treasured now as a symbol of all the doctors who died there.

Altogether sixty-five doctors died in the Memphis epidemic, forty of them Tennesseans. "They were all heroes," one historian summarized the doctors' work. "Every call was obeyed, no matter at what hour it came, or from whom."

It was the fifth yellow fever epidemic that Memphis had suffered in fifty years, and only five years before over two thousand people had died of the disease. The very name "yellow jack" struck such terror that the one thought was to escape the city. Whole families rushed out of their homes in such panic that they left the doors open and the curtains fluttering at the windows. They clawed each other for seats or standing room on the train, and fear-crazed men crashed through windows to crawl over the laps of lady passengers.

Men deserted their wives and children to escape the disease that no doctor had been able to explain. Some doctors theorized that the disease rose from the "foul gases" steamed from broken pavement, and others blamed the fever on the public "filth" that a corrupt political machine was responsible for. Poor sewerage, they said, meant yellow fever.

But as the disease boiled to a furious virulent form, citizens from the wealthiest homes, the most beautifully kept streets, died as frequently as those from the slums. Filth did not explain the disease.

Medical men and sanitation officers did observe that the riverboats that brought stricken crews to Memphis often had slimy bilge water. They ordered the boats cleaned up, but they never suspected that the bilge water was breeding ground for the deadly mosquito that spread the disease.

It was not until twenty-two years later, in 1900, that that riddle was solved. Dr. Walter Reed, in heroic experiments in Cuba, proved that yellow fever can be transmitted from one patient to another only by the bite of a mosquito, the *Aedes aegypti*. Once the mosquito has bitten a yellow fever patient, the insect can infect every person it bites as long as it lives.

But the doctors of 1878 had no way of knowing the cause. Some said that lack of "ozone" in the air was to blame, and the stormless summer had cut down on ozone. Comparing weather records for all the years when yellow fever had struck, they found unusually high humidity, unusual heat. They studied the geography of the disease as it moved up the Mississippi River from New Orleans as far north as Saint Louis and Cincinnati, and they knew that yellow fever was "river borne."

Yet the disease followed the main railroad lines, too. When refugees from the New Orleans epidemic got off the trains at small towns along the way, those towns soon became infested with the disease. Incoming passengers, luggage, and freight were "fumigated" to remove all "poisonous gas," but even when infected boats pulled up at a quarantined dock and no passengers were allowed to get off, yellow fever popped up over town anyway.

Doctors observed that cool weather always brought an end to yellow fever epidemics, and noticed that the spread of the disease seemed to have something to do with the wind currents. They unwittingly described precisely the conditions under which mosquitoes thrive.

Terrified, the citizens fled Memphis by river, train, wagon, buggy, and foot. Parents abandoned their small children to flee the fever, and highly respected citizens resorted to barbaric tactics to save their own lives.

When all who could escape the city had done so, there were fewer than nineteen thousand left, about a third of the normal population. Many of those who stayed behind were the city's poorest citizens—the Irish immigrants and the Negroes who had poured into Memphis from cotton plantations all over the Delta after the Civil War.

Of the approximately nineteen thousand who stayed in Memphis, all but two hundred had the fever. Out of every ten white persons who had the fever, more than seven died. For a long time Negroes were believed immune to the disease, but as it became more virulent, they too fell victim. Still, less than one out of every fifteen Negroes who had the fever died.

At the end of the two-month ordeal of blood, sweat, and unspeakable suffering, 5,150 people had died within the city. Hundreds more died after they fled Memphis.

The fourteen thousand Negroes who stayed in the deserted city relaxed at first in the sure knowledge that food would be doled out free at the supply depot, and in the belief that they were immune to the dread yellow killer, yet eventually 960 of them died. The Negroes were heroes, too. Many of them stayed on to nurse the stricken white people, and many others were organized into an emergency police force to protect the deserted city from looting and crime. They bolted the windows of empty homes, and patrolled the city day and night. They reported new cases of illness found on their rounds, and they reported bodies to be buried.

The whole city was under a sort of private martial law. The "Howards," an organization formed in an earlier yellow fever epidemic to provide medical care for all victims and maximum protection for all the city, worked closely with the board of health to distribute doctors, nurses, medicine, food, police protection, and burial for the city in agony. They had tons of disinfectant sprayed on the pavement, and the already smelly streets were fumigated with piles of burning sulphur. They even fenced off a street where one of the first victims died, in the hope that others would not come near the "poison gases" that were believed to be flying through the air.

Carefully the doctors plotted the course of the disease— the route it took up alleys and across streets, then suddenly skipping past unblighted homes to wipe out whole neighborhoods blocks away.

The "Black disease" that changed the whole history of Memphis began on July 15, 1878, when a Negro named Black Robinson made a trip down the river to Moon's Landing on the steamer *Osceola Belle*. When he returned to Memphis on July 21, he was sick and went at once to the home of a Mrs. Ferguson where his wife was cook.

There, in the little alley-side quarters where they lived, he recovered from the grave illness that turned out to be yellow fever. In a few days Willy Darby, a young boy who passed through the alley every day on his way to work at a saloon, became ill with yellow fever. He recovered too, but in less than a month six people whose homes were ranged along the alley had died of yellow fever.

It was the nightmare that Memphis had dreaded since the preceding May, when a yellow fever epidemic broke out in the West Indies. New Orleans slapped a quarantine on all ships from the Indies, but somehow the steamer *Sudder* slipped through quarantine on May 23 with a sick purser aboard. He died in New Orleans, and the epidemic that took 3,960 lives in that city and 21,000 in the Mississippi Valley had begun.

River towns looked with horror on every boat arriving from New Orleans. Memphis citizens demanded a quarantine that would keep all boats and trains from the Louisiana metropolis at a distance. Even Nashville newspapers kept an eye on news of the slow progress of the fever up the Mississippi. On Thursday, August 1, the Nashville *Daily American* reported: "Not a single case has yet reached the city."

Two weeks later Memphis was thrown into a state of panic by the announcement that there were twenty-two new cases of yellow fever in the city and two patients had died the day before. It was on August 14 that the stampede to the railroad stations took place, and four days later twenty thousand people had fled the city. Camps were set up several miles from the city for those citizens too poor to "refugee," and strict laws of quarantine were enforced among them.

By the last week in August, only those unable to get away from the city were left. Three thousand of them were ill with the ghastly fever.

"An appalling gloom hung over the doomed city," one survivor reported. "At night, it was silent as the grave. By day, it seemed desolate as the desert. There were hours, especially at night, when the oppressions of universal death bore upon the human mind as if the day of judgment was about to dawn. Not a sound was to be heard. At midday a noisy multitude of Negroes broke in upon the awful monotony of death clamoring each for his dole of the bounty which saved the city. When these had gone to their homes, the cloud of gloom closed down again and settled thick, black and hideous upon every living soul."

Crackpots advertised every "remedy" from applying "liver pads" to abstaining from tobacco. But no doctor pretended to have the answer to the revolting disease that flattened strong men with fever up to 106 degrees and left them so weak that they might drop dead from the effort of reading a newspaper.

Memphis doctors, working around the clock and meeting every night to compare notes, died in such numbers that physicians from Alabama, Indiana, Ohio, Georgia, Arkansas, Texas, New York, Missouri, Kentucky, and Louisiana volunteered their services to the prostrate city. Stories of the thousands of sick and dying in the steamy bluff city stirred the sympathy of the world, and donations of food, clothing, and medicine poured into Memphis from all over the United States, France, England, Germany, India, Australia, and South America. Men and women from all over the country volunteered to go to Memphis and nurse the helpless patients, and many of the volunteer nurses fell victim to the disease and were buried there.

Some of the volunteer "nurses" turned out to be racketeers—men and women who came into the homes of the wealthy ostensibly to nurse them but actually to ransack their homes of jewelry, silver, and other valuables. Some of the "nurses" who died on duty left suitcases crammed with the loot they had stolen from their "patients."

Whiskey, beer, and brandy were prescribed for the patients, both to drink and to bathe in, and a sympathetic nation donated trainloads of the stimulants to the city. They were furnished all fever victims without charge, and in great quantities. Racketeering "nurses" swarmed over the city to help themselves to the liquor rationed to their patients, and orgies of drunkenness and wantonness among "nurses" who deserted their patients added the final shocker to the macabre scene.

The sheriff, who a few days later died of the fever himself, issued orders that all nurses who were found drunk on the streets or who deserted their patients be thrown into jail. But the jailers, too, died.

The hot, dank days were filled with gruesome stories, like that of the wife of one of the city's prominent citizens. The day that her husband died and was carted off for a hurried burial, the woman lay in a raging fever. That night her drunken nurse deserted her, and the delirious woman rose from her bed, removed all her clothes, and wandered through the city's streets and on out the long road to the cemetery, constantly calling her husband's name, searching for his grave in the chilly darkness.

Whole households were discovered with as many as nine bodies to be buried, and the most welcome gift the city received was a trainload of coffins. Gravediggers collapsed from working day and night, and bodies were stacked in rows waiting their turn at burial.

No funeral services were held, for members of a bereaved family were usually unconscious or too weak to leave their beds. All clothing and bedding were burned immediately, and the living could tell where the latest deaths had been by the little black mound of ashes in the street in front of each stricken home.

Scores of bodies were found on the streets, in empty homes, in closed stores, and many of them were buried without identification. The loathsome disease so disintegrated the body that identification was often impossible. The lemon-yellow color of the victims' skin gave it its more usual name, and the variation, yellow jack. Dr. Summers, of Nashville, was in charge of the research work in Memphis, and he conducted hundreds of autopsies.

The wagons that hauled bodies off to the cemeteries broke down under the strain. There was no time for marking graves, and many of the wealthiest citizens were buried in the paupers' cemetery. When the epidemic was over, survivors wandered up and down the rows of thousands of new graves, stunned at the realization that they would never know which held the bodies of their families.

All social distinction vanished under the common woe. Annie Cook, "after a life of shame," died a heroine and won high praise in editorial columns. She had turned her house of ill fame over to medical authorities to be used as a hospital, and she herself nursed patients until she died of the fever.

Businessmen who had once been highly respected were disgraced after they deserted their stricken families. Ministers who deserted their congregations were shunned as cowards from that day, while Catholic priests and nuns who ministered not only to the large Catholic population but also to Protestants died by the dozens and showed the world the strength of their belief.

By September 14 the epidemic had boiled to its climax, with 127 deaths that day. Many of the relief workers who had predicted their own deaths three days before were dead.

Health officers, doctors, the chairman of the relief committee, and managers of the supply depot were dead.

But from that date, the number of new cases and deaths began to taper off. In the last week of September, for the first time in weeks, there were fewer than a hundred deaths a day.

The disease had spilled over from Memphis to take lives throughout Tennessee—193 in Chattanooga, 140 in Brownsville, 60 in Grand Junction, 53 in Somerville, 42 in Germantown. By enforcing a sensational "shot-gun quarantine," Jackson escaped with only three deaths.

On September 22, Dr. Summers, "who has prepared a full report of his discoveries for publication," left Memphis to make a report to Washington, the *Daily Appeal* reported. On that date the paper reported Dr. Bartholomew "convalescing." On September 27 the paper reported that he was back on duty in the fourteenth civil district. "There have been a great many cases of fever in this district," the paper stated, "and Dr. Bartholomew reports the type malignant."

On October 8 the paper reported that "Dr. Bartholomew of Nashville . . . a relapse case . . . was stricken with the fever." That same day he died, and rare tribute was paid him in all Memphis newspapers.

"Modest and unassuming, but skillful and energetic, he gave up his life in the cause of humanity, a hero-martyr, canonized in the affections of the people he came to save from the fate he met so bravely," said the *Daily Appeal*, and the *Daily Memphis Avalanche* reported that Dr. Bartholomew's death was marked by a rare tribute: a funeral was held.

Back in Nashville (where only ten persons died of the fever, and they were refugees from Memphis), Dr. Summers wrote his authoritative book, *Yellow Fever*, dedicating it to Dr. Bartholomew and two other former medical students who died in the Memphis disaster. Describing all circumstances and aspects of the disease, Dr. Summers all but pinpointed the cause. Yet he was so baffled that his only solution was to evacuate a stricken city.

The epidemic of 1878 was a turning point in Memphis' history, because many of the most important citizens who fled to Saint Louis, Cincinnati, and Atlanta never returned. For a long time afterward the greater part of the population was made up of Negroes and poor Irishmen who survived.

The cultural life of the city came to a complete halt. The city government was bankrupt. Atlanta became the center of the southeastern area of the United States because both government agencies and private industry were afraid to settle in Memphis.

The city, devastated and impoverished as if in battle, made slow recovery. Even now, Memphians date their history not before and after the Civil War, but before and after "the fever" of 1878.

The Mystery
of the Melungeons

Who are the Melungeons, the "mystery race" tucked away
between giant ridges of East Tennessee mountains long
before the first white explorer arrived? What exotic tale
of shipwreck or mutiny lies in the dark eyes of the red-
brown people already in Hancock County before Daniel
Boone cut a trail? What story of explorers strayed from De
Soto's party four hundred years ago or of Portuguese sailors
stranded on the North Carolina coast stares out in their
steady gaze?

A photographer and I set out to talk to these shy people
and, if possible, to break down their long-standing refusal to
have their picture taken. In part, we succeeded.

We found that the dark people are indeed there, pocketed
mysteriously in the mountains where tow-headed Anglo-
Saxon children fill most of the schools. But the sullen eyes of
Anglo-Saxon citizens (who make up 99 percent of the population of Hancock County) followed every move we made,
and even the sheriff challenged the photographer's right to
take a picture of the courthouse. The tragedy of the "lost
race" was thick around us.

"Every eye in the valley is watching you," one of our
kind guides (who asked not to be identified) said after we
had left Sneedville, the county seat, and risen over Newman's
Ridge to dip down the back side where the few identifiable
members of the race live. "It's not just the Melungeons. It's

the other people who resent what outsiders have written about our county."

So deep is the resentment in Hancock County against inquiring outsiders, particularly against certain Knoxville newspapers and the *Saturday Evening Post* for stories they published, that all writers and photographers are under suspicion.

The truth is that Melungeons are a vanishing race, a race so rare that Hancock County citizens can point out only two or three families with certainty. And they prefer not to do that. For the word Melungeon (pronounced Me-*lun*-jun) itself is so clouded in tragedy that people there will not say it.

A much maligned people, not white or black or yellow or red, the Melungeons had to take their case to the Tennessee Supreme Court before the Civil War to win the decision that they were not Negroid and were therefore entitled to send their children to school with white children. Before that, in the state constitution of 1834, they were disfranchised as "free men of color" and were denied the right to sue or testify in court. White men who coveted the rich lowlands the Melungeons had cultivated pushed them off their acres and onto the rocky ridges. The Melungeons had no recourse.

Trapped in poverty, snubbed by their fair-skinned neighbors, some of them withdrew to the poor land along Snake Hollow, deep in the rattlesnake-infested gorge in the shadow of towering Newman's Ridge. Some of them settled along the northern end of the valley, at the Virginia line, where Blackwater Creek flows, and some settled on the Ridge.

"I have never heard one refer to himself as a Melungeon," Mildred Haun, gifted Tennessee writer who grew up in a neighboring county and wrote many stories about them, said. "Most of the mountain people refer to them as Blackwaters and Ridgemanites."

Even in that long gorge, winding some twenty miles in a half-mile-wide band between Newman's Ridge and Powell Mountain, there are few "pure Melungeons" left today. The Melungeons still there deeply resent outsiders who pry into their ancestry and pontificate on their intelligence and industry. They themselves refuse to discuss the matter, and few will talk to reporters on any subject. They and fellow citizens of Hancock County are incensed at busloads of brash teachers and students from university sociology classes who descend on the courthouse from time to time to announce they are "looking for Melungeons."

Miss Martha Collins, vice-president of the Citizens Bank of Sneedville, sat at her trim-lined desk in the air-conditioned, modernistic bank and pondered questions we asked her. Obviously it was not a subject to dismiss lightly, or to discuss with strangers who might write misleading stories. A fair-skinned, blue-eyed woman whose calm efficiency in running the bank was sharpened in twenty-five years of training under her distinguished father's presidency, Miss Collins weighed her words and spaced her sentences as precisely as figuring interest.

"I used to regard the stories about Melungeons as a part of mythology," Miss Collins, a college graduate who is descended from one of the oldest families in the region, said. "But my sister said, 'No, there is some truth in it.'"

Miss Collins rose from her desk and walked thoughtfully to the vault to withdraw a letter postmarked 1907. It had been written to her by one of her uncles. Elegant in vocabulary and charming in sentiment, the letter related some of the family stories about the Melungeons' origin.

Written by J. G. Rhea, the letter told of one of the legends that persists to explain the presence of the dark-skinned people in the area: they are descendants of the Spaniards and perhaps Portuguese men in De Soto's party who ventured from Florida into parts of North Carolina and Tennessee in search of gold in 1540. According to this story, some of the men became lost from De Soto's party, were either captured or befriended by Cherokee Indians, intermarried with them, and left their descendants in Rhea, Hawkins, and Hancock counties in Tennessee and neighboring counties in Virginia.

"Navarrh Collins . . . a fine old patriarch . . . said to be of Portuguese descent, was one of the early settlers," Rhea wrote. "He settled on Blackwater Creek and owned Vardy Mineral Springs." Vardy, a community centered around a neat cluster of white-frame church, school, and missionary-teacher's residence, got its name from Spanish settlers, tradition says. *Navarrh*, Rhea said, was a variation of *Navarre*, a region in Spain. When Navarrh Collins opened Navarrh Mineral Springs, a long-ago health resort in the valley, the name was soon contracted to *Varr* and then *Vardy*.

There is nothing of the backwardness of the traditional mountaineer in the letter, and it is obvious that Hancock County has—and for generations has had—its aristocracy, some of whom took pride in their Spanish and Portuguese ancestry as well as in their Scotch-Irish blood. But there are no Spanish or Portuguese names in the community now, and there is no peculiarity of vocabulary to set the Melungeon apart from other citizens of comparable education and background.

The late Mrs. John Trotwood Moore, historian and former head of the Tennessee State Library, said original family names of the Melungeons disappeared as they took the names of English-Irish settlers who came into the mountains after the Revolutionary War. The Melungeons became Collinses, Mullinses, Gibsons, Freemans, Goinses, and so on. Others may have anglicized their Spanish and Portuguese names.

The Melungeons themselves, a clannish lot who are said to talk freely among themselves of their mysterious beginnings, are silent when outsiders broach the subject. Miss Collins, at the Sneedville bank, had told us we might find one of the dark-skinned people some fourteen miles away, where Snake Hollow Road crooks through the shadowy gorge between Sneedville and Tazewell. Mrs. Bertha Bell, Miss Collins said, might talk to us and pose for our photographer.

Mrs. Bell did both, chatting happily on every subject from gardening to taxes, until the origin of the settlers was mentioned. A slight, engaging woman, hospitable and kind, she became as inscrutable as Buddha when we asked her about Portuguese or Spanish settlers in the area, and finally about Melungeons.

"I don't know anything about that," she said, suddenly wide-eyed and innocent. "I don't know about such as that."

Her skin had the red-brown color of an Asiatic. Her bare feet, after fifty-eight years of walking the rocky roads unshod, were dainty and shapely. Her hands and feet had none of the light coloring of Negro palms and soles. It was a reminder of telling evidence used by one of Tennessee's early lawyers of distinction, John Netherland, to win the lawsuit hinging on the fact that Melungeons are not Negroid.

Some observers say the distinct coloring of a Melungeon does not blend with that of a white. Some of the children of mixed marriages are white, while others have the red-brown coloring of the Melungeons. White mothers, for instance, may have dark sons and white daughters.

The setting for tragedy is complete. The dark forebodings and heartbreak that come of the mixed marriages is theme of many of the short stories in the remarkable volume *The Hawk's Done Gone* that Mildred Haun published in 1940. In one story, she told of a white girl who did not know that her father was Melungeon. When she married and bore a dark-skinned child, the girl's husband killed both mother and child.

"From my observations and from all I have heard, I don't believe they blend in color," Miss Haun, a writer for the Department of Agriculture in Washington, D.C., said. But some lifelong residents of Hancock County say Melungeons do indeed blend with other races. For centuries they kept their distinctive look because they were so isolated that they seldom married outside their clan.

The name Melungeon is said to come from the French word *melange*, meaning "mixture." But that, too, is conjecture. Another explanation is that the word comes from *melas*, a Greek word meaning "dark," and that fits the theories of the ancient Greek beginnings of the race. Still another explanation is that the word comes from an Afro-Portuguese word, *melungo*, meaning "sailor."

It is the Portuguese sailor tradition that persists among the Melungeons. Those who discuss the matter simply say they are "porter-ghee." According to them, some time before the American Revolution, Portuguese sailors mutinied, and their ship was beached off the coast of North Carolina. The sailors came ashore only to encounter hostile Indians, and when they had killed the Indian men, they claimed the Indian women as their own.

One version of this story is that some of these Portuguese sailors were descended from ancient Phoenicians who had moved from Carthage to Morocco, from where they crossed the Strait of Gibraltar to settle in Portugal. "A colony of these Moors is said to have crossed the Atlantic and settled in North Carolina," the *Encyclopedia Americana* states.

Chinese sailors were known to have made their way to Portugal and intermarried with the Portuguese. That slightly oriental strain is one of the clues to the slant eyes and silky skin of some of the Melungeons.

One thing is sure: the mystery is alive and walking in Hancock County.

As Mrs. Bell stood on the front porch of her home—the only two-story house on narrow Snake Hollow Road—her nine-year-old grandson, Terry, appeared around the corner of the house. His dreamy oriental eyes and elfin face held all the mystery of his race. Like one of the genies from the *Arabian Nights*, the long-legged boy scampered over rocks and around tree roots, bouncing the "wheelbarrow" he had created by nailing the lid of a tin bucket to a long stick.

"All it takes to make a boy happy in this part of the country is a hammer and some nails," his grandmother commented happily.

The boy grew quiet at the sound of a jet plane zooming far above the mountain that walls in his world, and he and his grandmother squirted tobacco juice thoughtfully.

"Not anything goes too fast for me," the boy of mysterious past said.

"And no water's too deep for a boy," his grandmother added, nodding her head till her string of pearls twinkled, with an animation no stoic mountaineer knows.

Why Are They Vanishing?

How the dark-skinned Melungeons found their way from some distant land into the deep pockets of East Tennessee mountains is one mystery. Where they are vanishing to is another.

Mrs. Bertha Bell, one of the few remaining examples of the dark people of Hancock County, had one explanation. Barefoot and charming, with pearls around her neck even as she made tomato juice, Mrs. Bell spoke of the young people who had moved away from her silent valley where Snake Hollow Road pokes its rocky way through thick clumps of wildflowers and shadowy forests.

"The young people today are lazy," she said, her brown eyes snapping and her gentle voice quick, animated in a way completely foreign to the typical mountaineer. "Thee are too lazy to walk seven or eight miles to the grocery store. Thee are moving out of the valley and off the mountain into town where thee can live near the grocery."

They was always *thee* in her vocabulary, and *yonder* was *yander*. *Potatoes* were *taters*, and *Maryland*, where one of her daughters lives, was *Murland*. She said she had never heard the romantic stories of Melungeons, of their descent from Portuguese sailors or Spanish explorers of four centuries ago.

Mrs. Bell, fifty-eight, has lived all of her life on Snake Hollow Road, deep in the gorge that lies at the foot of Newman's Ridge, near the Virginia line. She loves the brilliant autumns when the mountainside at her back door is a blaze of red and yellow leaves, and the creek where she used to wade as a child is swift.

She worries about the changes the outside world is making in their way of living. Nimble as a schoolgirl, she thinks nothing of trotting seven miles to the nearest mill with a sack of corn to be ground into meal. But electricity threads the mountains and valleys now, and television antennas sprout out of the lonely cabin roofs like giant briars to trap the outside world. Even her crippled son, Venus, who lives just up the creek, can follow the day's news the moment it is flashed across the world. Washing machines sit proudly on almost every front porch, as a sort of status symbol, and refrigerators—sometimes in the bedroom—are making ice cubes of spring water.

Melungeons, like many of the other citizens of Hancock County, have broken out of the rigid trap of a region that has never had a railroad and had few highways to lift them over the fierce barrier of the mountains until recent years. One theory is that with more travel to outside areas, they are intermarrying with whites so frequently that their distinctive characteristics are vanishing, and the Melungeon will soon be a relic of the history books. But some Melungeons still live four miles from the nearest road of any kind, and only last winter one desperately ill woman was brought down the steep mountain slopes by sled to the bright new hospital in Sneedville.

One of Mrs. Bell's sons, Archie, lives less than a quarter mile from her home, but he drives forty miles to his job in a Morristown lumber yard every day. His commuting is probably prelude to the step that a number of other valley people have taken: moving to Knoxville, Nashville, Baltimore, or other industrial centers for jobs.

Archie and his wife have eight children, ranging in age from seventeen years to four months. Their fine European features and wide variety of pigmentation are tantalizing—so concrete in their evidence of a mysterious past, so baffling in actual information.

As with most Melungeon women, the daughters of the family have a soft, round-faced beauty—in striking contrast to the lean-faced, bony look many mountain women of Anglo-Saxon descent have. Some of the Bell girls are fair-skinned, with dreamy brown eyes and black wavy hair. Some of them have blue eyes, pale golden skin, and pale reddish hair, and some have the straight black hair of the Cherokees. Some of the children have the red-brown skin of the Asiatics, with wavy, black hair. The father of the family, tall and lean, as most Melungeon men are, has the clean-cut features of a European, but his skin is quite dark.

Thomas Zachary, energetic and popular young graduate of the University of Tennessee, grew up in Sneedville and has always been fascinated with the exotic bit of Tennessee history represented by the dark people pocketed surprisingly in the region of tow-headed Anglo-Saxons. Zachary teaches in a one-teacher school called Ramsey, on Snake Hollow Road, in what was once a dense settlement of Melungeons. Most of the children in his classes are of obvious Scotch-Irish and English descent, but he makes the most of the region's odd grip on history. When geography classes are studying nations of Europe, he describes the blond Nordics as looking "something like little Julia here," or the dark-skinned people of southern Europe, including Spain and Portugal, as looking "something like olive-skinned Woodard."

But pride in their background grows slowly in these children. Even during World War II, dark-skinned Melungeons were classified as Negroes when they reported for military duty, and they had to get Hancock County officials to sign affidavits stating that the state supreme court had officially classified them as "non-Negroid." That problem has been complicated by the fact that some Melungeons, notably a colony that moved to Roane County, did intermarry with Negroes and did introduce a Negroid strain in certain instances.

In this Republican part of the state, the whole area smarted when Democrats taunted all opposition by calling them "Melungeons" in campaigns of long ago. The word, at least to some of them, remains an epithet.

Hancock County citizens descended from fine Virginia and South Carolina families have boiled in anger when ignorant outsiders referred to the whole county as "Melungeon."

"In 1947, when the *Saturday Evening Post* published an article about Melungeons in our county, it was so misleading

that college girls from Sneedville were called 'Melungeon,' "
Charles M. Turner, mayor of Sneedville and owner of the
town's largest drugstore, said. "It ruined college for them,
and one of the girls came home in tears and never returned
to get her degree."

But there has been a time when Melungeons took pride in
their ancestry and in the special skills of their race—working
in timber and precious metals, for instance. Dixon Merritt,
one of the authors of *A History of Tennessee and Tennesseans*, said recently that a colony of Melungeons was im-
ported to Wilson County about 1830 to work for a lumber
mill, and they stayed there until 1870. Some of them have
descendants there still.

"They took pride in being Melungeons," Merritt said.
"They traced their ancestry to the Phoenicians and said their
skill in working in timber and metal had been handed down
through the centuries, father to son."

One of the bizarre stories about early Melungeons,
doubted by some historians, is that they at one time manufactured counterfeit gold and silver coins in the East Tennessee region. It is known that silver was at one time abundant
on Straight Creek and is still found in Hancock County.
Mildred Haun, skilled fiction writer who grew up in a county
near Hancock and wrote *The Hawk's Done Gone* about the
region, said she had always heard of the Melungeons' skill
with gold and silver, though she had never heard of their
making coins.

"I have heard, and just accepted as a fact, that they were
especially good at making jewelry from gold, and that they
were the best silver-bullet makers when there were witches in
the country," Miss Haun said.

She remembered other skills of Melungeons—weaving
chair bottoms, for instance. "When I was about nine years

old, my grandmother had an old man come from Hancock County and spend two or three days and nights with us to bottom up all the chairs," Miss Haun said. "Before he came, she explained to me that he had black-colored skin and was different from some folks and that some people called him a Melungeon. This man, whose only name was Noah, was a real artist in bottoming chairs. I had a little straight chair and a little rocker which he said he could make pretty for the little girl. He split the splits into tiny string-size strips and wove them in a special design that turned out to be a rough outline of a tree in the rocker and a star in the straight chair."

When John Sevier organized the State of Franklin (fore-runner of Tennessee) in 1784, he found, in the high ridges of Hancock and Rhea counties, a "colony of dark-skinned, reddish-brown complexioned people," supposed to be of Moorish descent, who were neither Indian nor Negro but who had fine European features and claimed to be Portu-guese. The Melungeons never took part in Indian wars, siding with neither Indians nor whites, Sevier said. They never shared Indian beliefs or rites, and are said to have revered the cross, the symbol of Christianity. They claimed frequent communication with the spirit world.

Miss Haun told of a Melungeon who lived in a smoke-house near her grandmother's Hamblen County farm in 1942 and "claimed they [the Melungeons] were in this country before any other race, having been lost on a ship and by chance coming to American shores and living all right until laws were made that didn't let them vote in South Carolina, and they moved to Hancock County."

Oddly enough, some of the burial customs of the Me-lungeons resemble those of Eskimos in Alaska who belong to the Russian Orthodox church. The Melungeons, like the Eskimos, build a small house over each grave, and their cemeteries look like miniature villages. Children in Snake Hollow even now see some of the Melungeon grannies scrambling across the hills on special occasions to observe secret rites over the graves—"Speaking in unknown tongues," the children say.

As in Europe, the Melungeons follow the casket to the grave on foot, and observe a year's mourning. They keep the little frame houses over the graves painted white, even while their own homes have no paint. And those small houses sometimes serve a practical purpose: sheltering moonshine whiskey.

Baptist and Methodist churches abound in Hancock County, and Presbyterians have done valiant missionary work among the Melungeons for generations. At Vardy, where Presbyterians built a school and church in the 1890s, so many people have been inspired to go to college that Melungeons have all but vanished from the area.

"Once they get a college education, they seldom come back," one of the former teachers said. "They go to Chicago, or other distant places where they can get good jobs and nobody will ever call them Melungeon."

Mrs. Bell, at the opposite end of the valley that twists along the base of Newman's Ridge, lives in a home that was built as a Presbyterian mission house. Generations of Melungeon children got their schooling and religious training there, and every summer carloads of people from Vardy make a sentimental journey to the spot.

There are stories of Melungeons who lived in mountainside caves when the first white settlers arrived, and numerous stories of violent deeds. But there is also a record of fine, intelligent Melungeons who helped found some of the county's schools and churches. Undoubtedly there was a wide range of ability and character in the "975 free men of color" listed in the region in the census of 1795.

In a part of Tennessee that has never had slaves, the presence of the dark-skinned people is all the more striking. There have never been more than fifty Negroes in Hancock County at any one time, Miss Martha Collins, vice-president of the Citizens Bank at Sneedville, said.

The dark deeds that used to bring Melungeons into town for "murderin' courts" are less and less frequent. The violent crimes that used to shock the county, crimes that grew more out of a childlike amorality than out of any malice, are less and less frequent. The Melungeons who used to sit on the fence around the courthouse square in Sneedville are no longer there.

Hancock County, with a population of 7,614, has fewer people than at the time of the Civil War, and has lost one-third of its population in the last twenty years. Sneedville, with a population of 800, has the well-scrubbed look of a town on the make. With TVA electricity, a countywide telephone system, a new sewage system, and one of the state's educational television stations, the county seat is scouting for industry.

Mayor Charles Turner, town druggist and civic leader, talked to this reporter in 1963 about the need to create better feeling between the Melungeons and their neighbors, and the need for attracting tourists to the wild, almost untouched mountain beauty.

"Why not do both at one time?" I asked. "Why not find an enterprising playwright to write a drama about the mystery people of Hancock County? It could give the Melungeons self-respect and give their Anglo-Saxon neighbors some insight into their problems."

The result was *Walk Toward the Sunset*, a two-hour drama written by Kermit Hunter and presented throughout the summer season since 1969 in a rustic outdoor theater on a hillside at the edge of town. Farmers and townspeople volunteered their work in building the log benches and stage. College students and townspeople produce the drama. The Melungeons of the area are always special guests—without paying.

And the Melungeons now take such pride in their heritage that they paint their mountain cabins and speak more freely to outsiders.

They remain a puzzle to ethnologists. But whatever the mystery of their origin, there is no mystery about their vanishing, Miss Martha Collins says.

"They have more or less just died out," she said. "The families have just eroded."

Philosophical, tolerant of Middle and East Tennesseans who have little understanding of the mountaineer, she pondered the inscrutable past. "Any mystery our people ever had is gone—or at least any way of solving it," she said. "We are all immigrants in this country. Whatever we are, we are—trying to do the best way we can."

Bibliography

Sam Houston and the Mystery of His Tragic Marriage

Allen, Elizabeth, of Gallatin, Tennessee, great-niece of Eliza Allen, wife of Houston. Interview with the author.

Bruce, Henry. *Life of General Houston, 1793-1863*. New York: Dodd, Mead, 1891.

Coffee, John. Papers, 1770-1916. Dyas Collection. Manuscript Section, Tennessee State Library and Archives, Nashville.

Conner, Juliana Courtney. Diary, 1827. Manuscript Section, Tennessee State Library and Archives, Nashville.

Crawford, Jane Douglass, of New York, granddaughter of Eliza Allen and her second husband, Dr. Elmore Douglass, of Gallatin, Tennessee. Interview with the author.

Fergusson Family Papers, 1824-1927. Manuscript Section, Tennessee State Library and Archives, Nashville.

Haggard, John, of Nashville, grandson of Dr. W. D. Haggard, Nashville physician who attended Houston. Interview with the author, 1962.

James, Marquis. *The Raven: A Biography of Sam Houston*. Indianapolis: Bobbs-Merrill, 1929.

Moore, John Trotwood. Papers. Houston letter to his father-in-law. Manuscript Section, Tennessee State Library and Archives, Nashville.

Peyton, Emily T. Peyton Family Papers, concerning Houston and his marriage to Eliza Allen. Manuscript Section, Tennessee State Library and Archives, Nashville.

Sullivan, Mrs. Eleanor Allen, of Nashville, great-niece of Eliza Allen, wife of Houston. Interview with the author.

Williams, Alfred M. *Sam Houston and the War of Independence in Texas*. Boston and New York: Houghton Mifflin, 1893.

Aaron Burr Was Framed

Abernethy, Thomas Perkins. *The Burr Conspiracy.* Gloucester, Mass.: Peter Smith Publishers, 1975.

Bassett, John Spencer, ed. *Correspondence of Andrew Jackson.* 7 vols. Washington, D.C., 1926-35.

Claybrooke, John Samuel. Collection. Claybrooke and Overton Papers, 1747-1894. Manuscript Section, Tennessee State Library and Archives, Nashville.

Coffee, John. Papers, 1770-1916. Manuscript Section, Tennessee State Library and Archives, Nashville.

Duncan, William Cary. *The Amazing Madame Jumel.* New York: Oxford University Press, 1954.

Fergusson Family Papers, 1784-1927. Manuscript Section, Tennessee State Library and Archives, Nashville.

Minnigerode, Meade. *Theodosia Burr Alston, 1783-1813: Lives and Times.* New York: Putnam, 1925.

Murdock Collection. Overton Papers, 1780-1851. In holdings of Tennessee Historical Society. Manuscript Section, Tennessee State Library and Archives, Nashville.

Schnachner, Nathan. *Aaron Burr: A Biography.* New York: Frederick A. Stokes, 1937.

Wandell, Samuel Henry. *Aaron Burr: A Biography.* Compiled from rare and in many cases unpublished sources. New York and London: C. P. Putnam's Sons, 1925.

Lincoya, Old Andy's Little Indian

Bassett, John Spencer, ed. *Correspondence of Andrew Jackson.* 7 vols. Washington, D.C., 1926-35.

Hubbard, David. Papers, 1807-1871. Poem by Henry Alexander Wise about Lincoya. Manuscript Section, Tennessee State Library and Archives, Nashville.

Hurja, Emil Edward. Collection, 1788-1953. In holdings of Tennessee Historical Society. Manuscript Section, Tennessee State Library and Archives, Nashville.

James, Marquis. *Andrew Jackson: The Border Captain.* Indianapolis: Bobbs-Merrill, 1933.

Pretty Peggy Eaton

Coffee, John. Papers, 1770-1916. Dyas Collection. In holdings of Tennessee Historical Society. Manuscript Section, Tennessee State Library and Archives, Nashville.

Donelson, Andrew Jackson. Papers, 1779-1943. Manuscript Section, Tennessee State Library and Archives, Nashville.

Eaton, Margaret L. O'Neale Timberlake. *The Autobiography of Peggy Eaton*. New York: Scribner's, 1932.

Hurja, Emil Edward. Collection, 1788-1953. Letters from John Henry Eaton to Andrew Jackson about scandal concerning Eaton's wife. In holdings of Tennessee Historical Society. Manuscript Section, Tennessee State Library and Archives, Nashville.

James, Marquis. *Andrew Jackson: The Border Captain*. Indianapolis: Bobbs-Merrill, 1933.

Murdock Collection. Overton Papers, 1780-1851. In holdings of Tennessee Historical Society. Manuscript Section, Tennessee State Library and Archives, Nashville.

"Black Horse Harry" Lee

Armes, Ethel. *Stratford Hall: The Great House of the Lees*. Richmond: Garrett and Massie, 1936.

Bassett, John Spencer, ed. *Correspondence of Andrew Jackson*. 7 vols. Washington, D.C., 1926-35.

Jackson, Andrew. Papers, 1825-35. Library of Congress, Washington, D.C.

Lee, Charles Carter. Collection. Letters to and from Maj. Henry Lee. Virginia State Library, Richmond.

Matthew Fontaine Maury and the Seas

Caskie, Jaquelin Ambler. *Life and Letters of Matthew Fontaine Maury*. Richmond: Richmond Press, 1928.

Clarke, Arthur C. "I'll Put a Girdle round the Earth in 40 Minutes." *American Heritage Magazine*, 9, no. 6 (October, 1958).

Corbin, Diana Fontaine Maury. *A Life of Matthew Fontaine Maury*. London: S. Low, Marston, Searle, and Rivington, 1888.

Hawthorne, Hildegarde. *Matthew Fontaine Maury: Trail Maker of the Seas*. New York and Toronto: Longmans, Green, 1943.

Lewis, Charles Lee. *Matthew Fontaine Maury: The Pathfinder of the Seas*. Annapolis: United States Naval Institute, 1927.

Maury, Matthew Fontaine. *Manual of Geography*. New York: University Publishing, 1885.

———. *Physical Geography*. New York: University Publishing, 1873.

———. *Wind and Current Charts*. Washington, D.C.: C. Alexander, Printer, 1853.

Wayland, John W. *The Pathfinder of the Seas: The Life of Matthew Fontaine Maury*. Richmond: Garrett and Massie, 1930.

Capt. William Driver and the Flag

Acraman, Rodney William, Fiji Island native, descendant of Driver. Interview with the author, September, 1968, about Driver in the

Fijis.

Belcher, Lady Diana. *Mutineers of the Bounty and Their Descendants in Pitcairn*. New York: Harper and Brothers, 1870.

Benz, Mrs. William W., of Nashville, granddaughter of Driver. Interview with the author, June 16, 1974.

Driver, William. Letter to his children, January 13, 1871, describing storm at sea and Pitcairn Island adventure. Letter to Bishop Quintard, 1873, asking permission to found new parish. Letter to his sons, Henry L. and Robert, August 10, 1876. Manuscript Section, Tennessee State Library and Archives, Nashville.

————. Ship's log, the *Charles Doggett*, sailing from Salem, Massachusetts, January 30, 1831. Manuscript Section, Tennessee State Library and Archives, Nashville.

Driver family Bible. With notes about family history and the Civil War. In collection of Mrs. William W. Benz, Nashville.

Driver papers. Clippings, correspondence, etc., in scrapbook of Mrs. William W. Benz, Nashville.

Maude, H. E. *In Search of a Home*. Washington, D.C.: Smithsonian Institution, 1959.

Roland, Mary Jane Driver. *Old Glory: The True Story*. New York: Printed for the author, 1918.

Steamboatin' Tom Ryman

Barton, Leslie Ryman. "Papa's First Boat, the Steamer *Alpha*," and a list of boats owned by Ryman. Typed, 1919.

Coggins, Daisy Ryman, daughter of Ryman. "The Benediction," "A Comparison: Druid Hills Kroger Grocery, Atlanta, 1953, and Hyman's Grocery, Nashville, 1901," "Early Life of My Father," "Lights on Character of My Father," "The Pontoon Bridge and the Elevator," "The Ryman Family History," "Thomas Green Ryman, 1841-1904: The World into Which He Was Born." Collection of Mrs. Elizabeth Jones, Atlanta.

Douglas, Byrd. *Steamboatin' on the Cumberland*. Nashville: Tennessee Book, 1961.

Henderson, Jerry. "Nashville's Ryman Auditorium." *Tennessee Historical Quarterly*, 27 (1968).

Huxtable, Ada Louise. "Only the Phony Is Real." *New York Times*, May 13, 1973.

Jones, Elizabeth C., of Atlanta, granddaughter of Ryman. Interview with the author. Letters to the author, August 18 and 26, September 13, and October 20, 1973, about the Ryman family.

————. Private collection. Includes photographs and clippings from Nashville *American*, May 18, 1902, Ryman's work on the river and for religion; *American*, December 24, 1904, Ryman dying and his obituary; Nashville *Banner*, December 24, 1904, tribute to Ryman; *Banner*, December 27, 1904, Ryman funeral.

Morton, M. B. "The Colorful Eighties in Nashville." Nashville *Banner*, no date, no. 5 in series, "Last Days of Real Steamboating on the Cumberland." Collection of Mrs. Elizabeth Jones, Atlanta.

Mount Olivet Cemetery, Nashville. Records.

Nashville City Directory, 1892 to 1915.

Proctor, Louise, of Augusta, Georgia, granddaughter of Ryman. Interview with the author, about the Ryman family.

Roundtree, Mrs. John A. "A Reconstruction Wedding: Mary Elizabeth Baugh and Thomas G. Ryman, 1869, as Told by 'Sis Tom.'" Collection of Mrs. Elizabeth Jones, Atlanta.

George Washington Sent Augustin Gattinger

Barclay, Robert Edward. Papers, 1854-1961. Letters from Gattinger. Manuscript Section, Tennessee State Library and Archives, Nashville.

Dury, James, great-grandson of artist George Dury, brother-in-law of Gattinger. Interview with the author.

Gattinger, Augustin. *Botanical Fragments*. Nashville, 1884.

———. *The Flora of Tennessee and a Philosophy of Botany*. Nashville: Press of Gospel Advocate Publishing, 1901.

———. *The Medicinal Plants of Tennessee*. Nashville: F. M. Paul, Printer, 1894.

———. *The Tennessee Flora, with Special Reference to the Flora of Nashville*. Nashville, 1887.

Gray, William P., 3900 Crestridge Drive, Nashville, once owner of Gattinger house and gardens. Interview with the author.

Hailey, Robert A. *Dr. Augustin Gattinger: The Pioneer Botanist of Tennessee*. Nashville: Cumberland Press, 1904.

Mayfield, Mrs. George, of Nashville, former neighbor of Gattinger. Interview with the author.

Mount Olivet Cemetery, Nashville. Records.

Oakes, Henry R. *A Brief Sketch of the Life and Works of Augustin Gattinger*. Nashville: Cullom and Ghertner, 1932.

Peabody College for Teachers Library. Records.

University of Tennessee Library, Knoxville. Records.

University of the South Library, Sewanee. Records.

Yellow Terror

Bartholomew, Dr. Olando Duff. "History of Tennessee Medical Society." No source, 1878.

Hicks, Mildred. *Yellow Fever and the Board of Health.* Memphis: Memphis and Shelby County Health Department, 1964.

Keating, John McLeod. *A History of the Yellow Fever: The Epidemic in Memphis in 1878.* Memphis, 1879.

Memphis *Daily Appeal,* May-November, 1878.

Memphis *Daily Avalanche,* May-November, 1878.

Memphis *Ledger,* May-November, 1878.

Menees, Dr. Thomas W., of Nashville. Interview with the author, with stories of horrors and heroes of the yellow fever epidemic.

Nashville *Daily American,* July-November, 1878.

Sternberg, George M. *Transmission of Yellow Fever by Mosquitoes.* Smithsonian Institution Annual Report. Washington, D.C., 1900.

Summers, Thomas Ormond. *Yellow Fever.* Nashville: Wheeler Brothers, 1879.

Tennessee Department of Health, Nashville. Vital Statistics, on yellow fever epidemics from 1828 to 1879.

The Mystery of the Melungeons

Adair, James. *The History of the American Indians.* London: E. and C. Dilly, 1775.

Avery, Louise, missionary-teacher at Vardy, Hancock County, Tennessee. Interview with the author.

Bell, Archie, father of large family of Melungeons on Snake Hollow Road, Hancock County, Tennessee. Interview with the author.

Bell, Bertha, mother of Archie Bell, on Snake Hollow Road, Hancock County, Tennessee. Interview with the author.

Cole, Dr. William, of University of Tennessee, Knoxville. Interview with the author; he classifies Melungeons as Croatan Indians.

Collins, Martha, vice-president of bank at Sneedville, county seat of Hancock County, Tennessee. Interview with the author; she has wide knowledge of Melungeons and their changing role.

Elmore, Edith, of Department of Public Welfare, Nashville. Interview with the author; she gave statistics on number of Melungeons in the state.

Gilbert, William Harlen, Jr. "Red Bones of Louisiana." *Social Forces,* May, 1946.

Graves, Bill, storekeeper at Vardy, Hancock County, Tennessee. Interview with the author, about habits and attitudes of Melungeons and their neighbors.

Grohse, William P., of Vardy, Hancock County, Tennessee. Interview with the author, comparing Melungeons with their neighbors.

Hale, Will T., and Merritt, Dixon L. *A History of Tennessee and Tennesseans.* Vol. 6. Chicago: Lewis, 1913.

Haun, Mildred. *The Hawk's Done Gone*. New York: Bobbs-Merrill, 1940.

Livesay, A. T., mail carrier in area of Hancock County, Tennessee, for thirty-five years, resident since 1902. Interview with the author, about Melungeons at Vardy and Newman's Ridge.

Merritt, Dixon, Tennessee historian, Lebanon. Interview with the author; he said that many Melungeons who migrated to Wilson County were excellent, highly skilled timber men.

Moore, John Trotwood, and Foster, Austin P. *Tennessee: The Volunteer State, 1769-1923*. 4 vols. Nashville: Clarke, 1923.

Stoves, Mildred, Nashville social worker. Interview with the author, about Melungeons of East Tennessee.

Turner, Charles M., druggist and mayor of Sneedville, county seat of Hancock County, Tennessee. Interview with the author; he did much to bring about peace between Melungeons and their neighbors.

Worden, William L. "Sons of the Legend." *Saturday Evening Post*, October 18, 1947.

Zachary, Tommy, teacher at Ramsey, Hancock County, Tennessee. Interview with the author; he did much to bring about understanding between Melungeons and their neighbors.

Index